PHP PROGRAMMING FOR BEGINNERS

Key Programming Concepts.

How to use PHP with MySQL and Oracle databases

SERGEY SKUDAEV

ISBN-10 : 1548980072
ISBN-13 : 978-1548980078

Table of Contents

Disclaimer

The information presented in this eBook is sold without warranty either expressed or implied. The author will hold no liability for any damages caused either directly or indirectly by the instructions contained in this book, or by the software products recommended for installation and usage.

Who Should Read This Book?

Those who wish to learn computer programming in PHP should be familiar with HTML, as a knowledge of HTML will be helpful in your efforts. This book is also for those who know other programming languages and wish to learn PHP as well.

PHP is a server-side scripting language executed on a web server, sending HTML pages to the browser. Included in the following are instructions for the installation of Apache Web Server, PHP, MySQL database, and phpMyAdmin script used for MySQL database administration. And please note that all of the above-mentioned software can be readily obtained and used free of charge.

Introduction

Programming in any computer language or script is not as impossible as one might think.

Perhaps you're thinking that being very good at math is a prerequisite to becoming a computer programmer, however, this is not necessarily so. The average person can master computer programming. In fact, a study revealed that, among immigrants, former musicians tended to make good programmers, probably because writing music is much like writing code.

In a sense, programming is like packaging something because programming language deals with variables that are used to hold different pieces of data. What is a variable? Think of a variable as you would a box for packaging. When you select a box, you must consider the size and nature of the item(s) being packaged.

Numbers, text strings, and objects are what comprise a computer program. A variable might contain whole numbers, fractions, or pieces or strings of text. A variable that contains a whole number is called an integer. A variable holding a number with a decimal point is called a float or double, while a variable holding a piece of text is called a string.

Computer programs begin with a variable declaration and, with some exceptions, the data type. For example, in C++ or Java, you must declare the variable name and exact data type. A variable name, in any computer language, must be only one word. It may contain alphabetical characters, numbers, and underscores. Often programmers use prefixes to show variable data types. For example, strName for a string data type or int_Account for an integer data type, and so on.

The integer, double, string, and date are all data types. Each data type requires a different "space" in the computer memory. For example, an integer occupies four bytes, or, because there are 8 bits to a byte, 32 bits—a bit being the smallest unit of information. A bit may contain a 0 or a 1. In the binary system 00000001 equals 1, 00000010 equals 2, 11111111 equals 256, or 2 to the 8th power. Four bytes can hold numbers from -2,147,483,648 to + 2,147,483,647.

A Double occupies 8 bytes. Huge numbers with decimals can be held in a double. A float occupies 4 bytes and can hold a number with decimals. When selecting a gift box for a diamond ring, you wouldn’t choose a yard-by-yard box because it wouldn't be a very efficient way to package a ring. Likewise, with variables, you'll want to declare the data types according to the space requirements for efficient use of computer memory.

When it is important that code lines are not broken in the script, but the page width does not allow for their display without breaking, I use <=> to indicate that this line of code is to be continued, uninterrupted, on one line uninterrupted.

Declaration of variables

A computer program starts with the declaration of variables. In PHP you do not have to declare a data type. A variable name in PHP is preceded with a $ sign. For example, $n=0; The string of text should be enclosed in either single or double quotation marks. For example:

```
$firstname='Alexander';
Or
$lastname="Makedonski";
$name="Alexander Makedonski";
```

As you may have noticed, a line of code in PHP is ended with a semicolon.

It's always good practice to add comments when writing code, as they will enable you to better understand the meaning later. Also, if someone else reads or modifies your code, comments may be helpful. Comments must be preceded by two back slashes or placed between asterisks and backslashes:

```
/* this is code comment */
//this is another code comment
```

All PHP code blocks start with a "<?php" tag and ends with "?>" tag.

Basic Operators

Any computer language uses operators to calculate or compare variables, most of which are self-explanatory. For example, PHP uses + (plus), - (minus), * (multiplication), / (division), %(modulo) and "=" the assignment operator.

Let's discuss the modulo operator. The modulo operator is used in finding the resultant remainder after one number has been divided into another. The following are a couple of examples to help you better understand:

The first example is 15 % 5 = 0. As you can see, 5 divides evenly into 15 with no remainder, so the result we get is 0. Now let's use 10 % 7 = 3 as our second example. Because 7 divides into 10 once and leaves a remainder of 3, our answer must be 3.

30 % 6 = 0 (30 - 5 * 6 = 30 30 - 30 = 0)
30 % 7 = 2 (30 - 4 * 7 = 30 - 28 = 2)
30 % 8 = 6 (30 - 3 * 8 = 30 - 24 = 6)

Comparison operators

$a == $b Equal TRUE if $a is equal to $b after type adjustment.
$a === $b Identical TRUE if $a is equal to $b, and they are of the same type.
$a != $b Not equal TRUE if $a is not equal to $b after type adjustment.
$a <> $b Not equal TRUE if $a is not equal to $b after type adjustment.
$a !== $b Not identical TRUE if $a is not equal to $b, or they are not of the same type.
$a < $b Less than TRUE if $a is strictly less than $b.
$a > $b Greater than TRUE if $a is strictly greater than $b.
$a <= $b Less than or equal to TRUE if $a is less than or equal to $b.
$a >= $b Greater than or equal to TRUE if $a is greater than or equal to $b.

Let's see an example with = = = identical operator.

```
$a = "10";
$b=10;
if ($a ==$b)
echo "a = b<br>";
else
echo "a <> b<br>";
If ($a === $b)
echo "a and b are identical<br>";
else
echo "a and b are not identical<br>";
```

Output:
a = b
a and b are not identical

$a and $b are equal because they equal 10, but they are not identical because $a is a string and $b is an integer.
$a = 9; Assignment: $a equals 9.
$a += 7; Addition-assignment: $a equals $a plus 7.

$a *= 4; Multiplication-assignment: $a equals $a multiplied by 4.

$a /= 3; Division-assignment: $a equals $a divided by 3.

$a.= 6; Concatenation-assignment: $a equals $a concatenated with 6

Let's write a simple code converting Fahrenheit to Celsius.

```
<?php
   // $F is a temperature in Fahrenheit, $C is
in Celsius
 $F=80;
    //The "echo" is a command that Output:s text
to
    //the browser
 echo "F= ". $F."<br>";
    // a formula to convert Fahrenheit to
Celsius
 $C = ($F - 32) * 5/9;
 //Output: temperature in Celsius
 echo 'C= '. $C.'<br>';
 ?>
```

Output:

F=80
C=26.6666666667

Please pay attention to "F= ". $F."
"on the code line echo; Here we concatenate 3 separate strings into one.

```
"F="
$F
"<br>" - HTML break.
```

Two dots are placed between our three strings because dots are used to concatenate strings in PHP:

```
"F=". $F. "<br>";
```

The fact is that $F is not a string. It is an integer because it is equal to 80. If $F were equal to "80" it would be a string.

When we concatenate the $F variable between 2 strings, because PHP converts it to a string, there is no need to do anything further.

As I wrote earlier, a string of text can be enclosed in single quotation marks:

```
echo 'F='. $F.'<br>';
```

To Output: a string of text, you can use the "print" command instead of the "echo" command.

However, in this case, you would use parentheses and single or double quotation marks.

```
print ('F= '. $F.'<br />');
Or
print ("F= ". $F."<br />");
```

PHP variables are case sensitive, so $F is not the same as $f, and $lastname is not the same as $Lastname or $LASTNAME.

Let us say that we wish to use PHP to Output: a web page to a browser using the following HTML link:

```
<a href="http://www.yahoo.com">yahoo</a>
```

If we write

```
print ("<a href="http://www.yahoo.com">yahoo</a>");
```

we would receive an error message due to the use of double quotation marks in our HTML code. To avoid the error message, use single quotation marks for the print command as I've done in the following:

```
print ('<a href="http://www.yahoo.com">yanhoo</a>');
```

The same is true for an HTML input element:

```
echo '<input type="text" name="lname"
value="James"/>';
or
print ('<input type="t0oext" name="fname"
value="John"/>');
```

One handy feature of the PHP code is the ability to include one file inside another. The creation of a website solely in HTML requires you to edit every single page of that website if you later wish to change the navigation, logo or footer. The use of PHP to create the web pages allows you to include one file with navigation or logo in every web page requiring you to edit only one file to later change the navigation or logo.

There are two commands to include the file in your PHP code:

```
include('top_menu.php');
or
require("footer.php");
or
require_once ("footer.php");
```

The difference between the two is, when using the "include" command, if the file to be included does not exist, you will be given a warning message; however, the execution of the rest of the PHP code will not be interrupted. Conversely, when using the "required" command, if the required file is not found, a fatal error message is displayed, and the execution of the PHP code will cease. The require_once is similar to the required ?? but it checks to include the footer.php file only once even if you write require_once ("footer.php"); twice.

Function

A function is a piece of code that performs a specific manipulation with variables and then returns the result from that manipulation. Functions are useful because they can be used multiple times over. There are PHP functions that are built-in, but a function can also be created by the user. Let's create one that converts Fahrenheit to Celsius. The PHP function declaration begins with the word function to be followed by the function name, which should be one word. Several parameters can be given to a function, but a function can only return one parameter in the return statement. Multiple parameters are enclosed together in parentheses and separated by comas. The entire piece of code inside a function is enclosed in curly brackets. In our example, we pass one parameter, a temperature in Fahrenheit, and return a temperature in Celsius.

```
function convertFtoC($F) {

$C = round (($F - 32) * 5/9);
return $C;
}
```

Now to convert Fahrenheit to Celsius you must call your function and pass the temperature in Fahrenheit.

```
$T= convertFtoC (80);
echo $T."<br>";
```

The Output: will be 27
The round is a built-in PHP function. It will round 26.6666666667 to 27.

Variable Scope

Variables in the PHP code may have different scopes. They may be seen or accessed globally, anywhere on the current php page or only inside the function. Let us analyze the following code:

```
<?php

 $greeting="Hello!";

 function greetme($name) {

 echo $greeting.' '. $name;
 }

 //function call
greetme('John');
?>
```

Output: John

At the beginning of the code, we assigned the "Hello" string to the $greeting variable. Then we defined the function with one parameter $name. Inside the function we concatenated the $name variable to the $greeting variable. Then we called the function and passed the name 'John' as a parameter.

You might expect the Output: would be "Hello John", since $greeting equals "Hello", but it's "John". "Hello" is not visible because the $greeting variable inside the function is not the same as outside. It's local, and because we assigned no value to the local variable $greeting, the value we passed as a parameter is the only one visible.

Let us modify the function.

```
<?php

$greeting="Good morning!";

function greetme($name) {

$greeting="Hi There";

echo $greeting.' '. $name;

}
```

```
echo greetme('John');
echo "<br>";
echo "Greeting= ". $greeting."<br>";

?>
```

Output:
Hi There John
Greeting=Good Morning

Inside the function we assigned the value "Hi There" to the local variable $greeting. As a result, the function will return "Hi There John". However, because we printed the $greeting variable outside the function, the global variable $greeting value remains "Good Morning".

Let us modify our code again.

```
<?php

$greeting="Good Morning";

function greetme($name) {

global $greeting="Hi There";

echo $greeting. ' '. $name;

}

echo greetme('John');

echo "<br>";

echo "Greeting= ". $greeting."<br>";

?>
```

Output:
Hi There John
Greeting=Hi There

In the above we've declared a global variable inside the function, using global. Then we assigned the value "Hi There" to the global $greeting variable.

We previously assigned "Good Morning" to the global variable $greeting outside the function. Then, inside the function, we assigned a global variable with the same name to the value "Hi There". Now the global variable $greeting no longer has the value "Good Morning", but rather "Hi There". So, when we print the value of the global variable outside the function it displays, "Hi There".

Static variable

A static variable is the same as a local variable, but it is not destroyed when the function execution is ended.

```
<?php

 function greetme($name) {

 static $greeting="Hi There";

 $greeting=$greeting.' '. $name;

 echo $greeting. "! <br>";

 }

 greetme('John');
 greetme('John');
 greetme('John');

 ?>
```

Output:
Hi There John!
Hi There John John!
Hi There John John John!

The value of the static $greeting variable is changing after each function call because the $name variable is added to it each time.

Remove the static keyword and the Output: of the function will be the same in the second and the third call

```
<?php

function greetme($name) {

$greeting="Hi There";
$greeting=$greeting.' '. $name;
echo $greeting. "! <br>";
}

greetme('John');
greetme('John');
greetme('John');
?>
```

Output:
Hi There John!
Hi There John!
Hi There John!

Passing parameters by value or by reference

At run time, the system assigns our declared variable to a memory location called a reference.

The reference to a variable can be accessed by preceding the identifier of a variable with an ampersand sign (&). The variable address is a hexadecimal number. As seen displayed in the following C++ code, on the first line we declare a pointer (*a) to a memory address. On the second line, we declare a variable (b) and assign its address to the pointer (a). And finally, on the last line, the content of the address of the memory location is displayed as a hexadecimal number.

```
int *a;
int b=7;
a = &b;
```

```
cout <<"The address of the memory location of
b:"<<a<<endl;
```

Output: The address of the memory location of b: 0039FF15

In PHP you can pass the variable address to a function by preceding its name with an ampersand (&). Normally, when we pass a variable to a function, by default the system makes a copy of the variable and passes the copy to the function. The value of the copy may change inside the function, but the value of the original variable remains the same.

As reflected in the two examples below, when passing a variable by reference, the address of the variable is passed inside the function. So, if a new value is assigned to the address, the value of the original variable changes as well. In the first example, we pass variables by values; and in the second, we pass them by reference.

```
<?php

function switch_by_value ($k, $n) {

$temp=0;
$temp=$k;
$k=$n;
$n=$temp;
}

$a = 5;
$b= 7;
echo 'By Value:<br>';
echo 'Before: a='. $a. ' b= '. $b.'<br>';

switch_by_value ($a, $b);

echo 'After: a='. $a. ' b= '. $b.'<br>';
?>
```

Output:
By Value:
Before: a=5 b=7

After: a=5 b=7

Notice that the values of the original variables (a) and (b) are not switched.

```
<?
 function switch_by_reference (&$k, &$n) {

 $temp=0;
 $temp=$k;
 $k=$n;
 $n=$temp;
 }

 $a = 5;
 $b= 7;
 echo 'By Reference:<br>';
 echo 'Before: a='. $a. ' b= '. $b.'<br>';
 switch_by_reference($a, $b);
 echo 'After: a='. $a. ' b= '. $b;

 ?>
```

Output:
By Reference:
Before: a=5 b=7
After: a=7 b=5

Notice that the values of the original variables (a) and (b) are switched.

Useful string functions

PHP has many built-in string functions. String length can be determined with strlen () function.

```
$lastname="Shakespeare";
$len=strlen($lastname);
echo "Length= ". $len."<br>";
```

Output: Length=11

The trim () function trims space characters from the beginning and the end of a string. This function is useful because a user may inadvertently enter space characters while typing in a login or password. To prevent this from occurring, trim every user input string as in the following example:

```
$lastname =' Shakespeare ';
echo "Before trim: ". strlen($lastname)."<br>";
$lastname=trim($lastname);
echo "After trim: ". strlen($lastname)."<br>";
```

Output:
Before trim 13
After trim 11

As you can see, I've intentionally entered a space at the beginning and end of the last name and its length became longer by two characters. After trimming these spaces, the length was restored to 11 characters.

The string position function **strpos ()** returns the position of the first occurrence of a substring in the string.

For example, echo strpos ($lastname, 'sp') will return 5.

You might expect it to return 6 because sp is in the 6th position; however, it returns 5

because the count starts at 0.

echo strpos ($lastname, 'Shake'); will return 0.

After execution, echo strpos ($lastname, 'shake'); nothing will be displayed in the browser because it returns Boolean false. Lower case 'shake' has not occurred in the 'Shakespeare'. To confirm this, execute the following code:

```
if (strpos ($lastname, 'shake')===false)

 echo "return false<br>";
```

Output: return false

The strpos is a case sensitive function. The **stripos** is a case insensitive function.

echo stripos ($lastname, 'shake'); will return 5.

The **strrpos()** - Find the position of the last occurrence of a substring in a string.
echo strrpos($lastname, 'e') will return 10.

The **substr ()** function will return a substring of a string.

echo substr ('William Shakespeare',8); will return Shakespeare

echo substr ('William Shakespeare',8, 5); will return Shake.

It starts counting from 0 and returns that piece of substring starting from the 8th character.
The second parameter, if it is present, determines the substring length. This explains why
echo substr ('William Shakespeare', 8, 5); will return Shake.

If the second parameter is not present, all that portion of string is returned.
This is why echo substr ('William Shakespeare', 8); will return Shakespeare
The **str_replace ()** is another important string function. This function replaces all occurrences of the search string with a replacement string.
For example, if a user enters text containing single or double quotation marks into a form, it can create problems with the database. To prevent this from happening, using the str_replace function, we can replace all occurrences of single quotation marks in the input text.

```
 $comments="this is comments with a 'single
quotation' marks";
 echo "before str_replace:". $comments."<br>";
 $comments=str_replace (" ' ", "&acute;",
$comments);
 echo "after str_replace:". $comments."<br>";
```

Output:
before str_replace: this is comments with a 'single quotation' marks after str_replace: this is comments with a ‘single quotation' marks

When viewing the web page source, you will see that each single quotation mark has been replaced by the ´ code.

PHP Array Functions

Arrays are used in any programming language. You can imagine an array as a long box with many identical compartments. Visualize it like this: |___|___|___|___|___|.

Whatever you place in a compartment is that particular compartment's value. Let's place the characters a, b, c, d and e in the following array of compartments: |_a_|_b_|_c_|_d_|_e_|

Now, to access any of these values, you'll need to know which compartment the value is stored in. For example, 'b' is stored in the second compartment.

In most computer languages, array index counting starts from 0, not 1, meaning that the index of the first element of the array is 0, the index of the second element of the array is 1 and so on. In the following array of names, you see the indexes and values:

//declare an array of names

```
$names=array ();

$names [0] ="John";
$names [1] ="George";
$names [2] ="James";
$names [3] ="Anna";
$names [4] ="Robert";
$names [5] ="John";
$names [6] ="James";
$names [7] ="George";
$names [8] ="Maria";
$names [9] ="Peter";
$names [10] ="James";
```

To display "Anna" you have to access the element (compartment) with the index 3. If you use the print command,

```
print ($names[3]);
```

The built-in function sizeof(array) returns the number of elements in an array. In this case,

```
$asize=sizeof($names);
```

Or you can use the count function

```
$asize=count($names);
```

To display all array values, we can use the for loop.
The for loop looks like this:

```
for ($i=0; $i<$asize; $i++)

print ($names [$i]."<br>");
```

In the for loop, the $i variable is incremented from 0 to the value one less than the $asize value. If the array has 11 elements, the $sizeof () function will return 11. The $i variable will be incremented to 10 and then stops. You might assume that if $i stops at 10, and we have 11 elements, the last array element would not be displayed.

However, that assumption would be wrong because the first array element index is 0, the eleventh element will have index 10, and so our code will display the element index 10, which is the 11th element of the array.

There are many useful built-in functions for arrays. The code below demonstrates some of these:

The in_array() function returns true if the value exists in an array.

So, in the above array of names, in_array('Anna') will return True, but in_array('Lidia') will return False.

The sort function sorts an array in ascending order.

The rsort function sorts an array in reverse order.

The array_pop function removes and returns the last element of an array.

The array_push function adds an element to the end of array.

The array_unique function removes duplicate values from an array.

The print_r function prints an array.

The array_rand function selects a random array element.

The implode function converts an array into a string.

```
<?php
print('<br>The sort function sorts array<br>');

 sort($names);

 //Get size of array
 $asize=sizeof($names);

 for($i=0; $i<$asize; $i++){
 //Check if it is female name put Mrs. prefix
 //else put Mr. prefix

 if(($names[$i] =="Anna")||($names[$i]
 =="Maria"))
     {
   print('Hello Mrs.'.$names [$i]."<br>");
      }
       else
      {
   print' Hello Mr.'.$names [$i]."<br>");
      }

 } //for

 print('<br>');
?>
```

Output:
The sort function sorts an array
Hello Mrs. Anna
Hello Mr. George
Hello Mr. George

Hello Mr. James
Hello Mr. James
Hello Mr. James
Hello Mr. John
Hello Mr. John
Hello Mrs. Maria
Hello Mr. Peter
Hello Mr. Robert

```
<?php
 echo "The array_unique function removes
duplicate array values<br>";

 $array=array ();

 $array=array_unique($names);

 foreach ($array as $key => $value) {

 echo $key . "-". $value . "<br>";
 }
 print('<br>');
?>
```

Output:
The array_unique function removes duplicate values.
0-Anna
1-George
3-James
6-John
8-Maria
9-Peter
10-Robert

```
<?php

rsort($array);

print("The rsort function sorts an array in
reverse order<br>");
```

```
 foreach($array as $key => $value) {
 echo $key . "-". $value . "<br>";
 }
?>
```

Output:
The rsort function sorts an array in reverse order
0-Robert
1-Peter
2-Maria
3-John
4-James
5-George
6-Anna

```
 <?php

print ('<br>The array_pop() function returns the
last element. <br>');
$lastelement=array_pop ($array);

print ('<br>The last element= '.
$lastelement.'<br>');
?>
```

Output:
The array_pop () function returns the last element
The last element=Anna

```
 print ('<br>Array after calling the array_pop().
 The last element removed. <br><br>');

 foreach ($array as $key => $value) {

 echo $key. "-". $value. "<br>";
 }
```

Output:
Array after calling array_pop (): The last element removed
0-Robert
1-Peter
2-Maria

3-John
4-James
5-George

The array_push function adds elements to the end of an array.

The print_r prints array function prints array key - value pairs.

```
<?php

array_push ($array, "Chris", "Colin");
print_r ($array);

?>
```

Array after calling array_push ($array, "Chris", "Colin") and print_r functions: Chris and Colin are added to the end of the array.

Output:
Array ([0] => Robert[1] => Peter[2] => Maria[3] => John[4] => James[5] => George[6]=> Chris [7] => Colin)

The array_rand($array) function returns random array index.

```
$random=array_rand ($array);

print ('<br>print array element by random index<br>');

print ('<br>Random element= '. $array [$random].'<br>');
```

Output:
print array element by random index
Random element=Colin

```
<?php
$string=implode ($array);
```

```
 print ("<br>Array is imploded in a
string:<br>");
 print ($string);
?>
```

Array is imploded in a string:
RobertPeterMariaJohnJamesGeorgeChrisColin

The for loop

```
for ($i=0; $i<10; $i++){
 print ($i."<br>");

}
```

The $i variable is local because it is defined inside the loop. However, if you try to Output: the $i variable outside the loop, its value will be 10.

Break and Continue

Break; statement breaks out of the loop. Loop execution stops.

```
 $names [0] ="Anna";
 $names [1] ="George";
 $names [2] ="James";
 $names [3] ="James";
 $names [4] ="John";
 $names [5] ="Maria";
 $names [6] ="Peter";
 $names [7] ="Robert";

 for ($i=0; $i <sizeof ($names); $i++) {

 if ($names [$i] == "John")
 Break;

 print ($names [$i]."<br>";
 }
```

The loop above will print the names:
Anna
George

James
James
and then stops. The names John, Maria, Peter and Robert will not be printed.

Continue; statement makes the loop skip iteration. See the following continue code example:

```
for ($i=0; $i <sizeof ($names); $i++) {

      if ($i == 0)
      print ($names [$i]."<br>");
      else
      {
         if ($names [$i-1] == $names [$i])
         continue;

      print ($names [$i]."<br>");
      }
}
```

Output:
Anna
George
James
John
Maria
Peter
Robert

In line if ($names [$i-1] == $names [$i]) we check if a previous name equals a current name. In the first iteration, we do not have a previous name, so we print a name without checking for a duplicate.

Starting from the second iteration, when $i = > 1 we check whether a previous name is equal to the current one. If it is, we skip the loop.

As a result, the duplicate name is not printed. The break and continue may be used in all other loops.

The foreach loop

To use the for loop for an array you have to know how many items the array has. Sometimes, it is more convenient to use the foreach loop. The Foreach loop has the following syntax:

foreach (array_expression as $value)
statement

http://php.net/manual/en/control-structures.foreach.php

If you have an array of names ($names) and you want to greet each person, use the foreach loop to avoid having to know how many names are in the array.

```
foreach ($names as $aname)
echo "Hello, ". $aname. "! <br>";
```

Output:
Hello, John!
Hello, George!
Hello, James!
Hello, Anna!
Hello, Robert!
Hello, John!
Hello, James!
Hello, George!
Hello, Maria!
Hello, Peter!
Hello, James!

In the foreach loop we can read and display not only a value of the array element but its key as well.

foreach (array_expression as $key => $value)
statement

```
foreach ($names as $key=>$aname)
echo $key." Hello, ". $aname. "! <br>";
```

Output:

0 Hello, John!
1 Hello, George!
2 Hello, James!
3 Hello, Anna!
4 Hello, Robert!
5 Hello, John!
6 Hello, James!
7 Hello, George!
8 Hello, Maria!
9 Hello, Peter!
10 Hello, James!

The number is the array element's index or key.

The while Loop

The 'while loop' is used in many programming languages. A code inside a while loop is executed while a condition is true.

When using the while loop, make sure that your condition will become false and the loop stops. Otherwise, you will be continuously stuck in the loop.

Let us print our array using the while loop.

```
while ($i < $asize) {

print ("Hello, ".name[$i]."<br />";

$i ++;

}
```

Output:
Hello, John!
Hello, George!
Hello, James!
Hello, Anna!
Hello, Robert!
Hello, John!
Hello, James!
Hello, George!

Hello, Maria!
Hello, Peter!
Hello, James!

If and if else statement

The if…else statement is used to execute different pieces of code under different conditions.

It has the following construction:

```
if (conditions) {
Do this.
}elseif (different condition) {
Do that.
}else {
Do something else.
}
```

Let us create a function that will print a message depending on temperature.

```
function weather ($F) {

if ($F > 78 )
$message="It is too hot!";
elseif ($F < 65 )
$message="It is too cold!"
else
$message="Today is nice outside!";
Return $message."<br />";
}
```

Let us call the function

```
echo weather (80);
```

Output: will be "It is too hot!";

```
echo weather (60);
```

Output: will be "It is too cold!";

```
echo weather (70);
```

Output: will be ="Today is nice outside!";

Switch statement.

The switch statement has the following syntax:

```
switch (variable) {
case label1:
code to be executed if variable =label1;
break;
case label2:
code to be executed if variable =label2;
break;
default:
code to be executed if variable is not equal any
label;
}
```

A Switch Example:

```
$temperature_C=100;

Switch ($temperature_C) {

Case: 0
$message="Water freezing point.";

Break;

Case: 100
$message="Water boiling point!":

Break;
Default:
```

```
$message="Neither freezing nor boiling point.";
}
```

If we pass in our switch statement variable with the value of 100 we will get Output: "Water boiling point!"

If we pass 0 we will get Output: ="Water freezing point."

Otherwise, we will get Output: "Neither freezing nor boiling point."

List

List is a language construction. It is used to assign a list of variables in one operation.

In the line below, I assign array $names from the array example above to a list of variables.

list ($name1, $name2, $name3, $name4, $name5, $name6) = $names;

print ($name5); will print John because it is the 5th name in the array.

Multidimensional Arrays

An example of a two-dimensional array is plane seats. A plane has rows identified by numbers and a few seats in a row identified by letters A, B, C, D, E, and F.

Let us imagine that we have 7 rows with 6 seats in each of the rows. Define an array of seats in a row as $s. Then in two for loops we can create an array of all seats.

```
$s=array ('A','B','C','D','E','F');

for ($i=0; $i <7; $i++) {

$row = $i+1;

for ($j=0; $j<6; $j++) {
$seats[$i][$j]=$row.$s[$j];

print($seats[$i][$j]);
```

```
if(($j % 5 ==0)&&($j>0))

print ('<br>');
    }
}
```

In an inner J loop, we assign a seat value to the two-dimensional array.

$row = $i + 1 because $i starts with 0 and the row starts with 1.

Then we concatenate a row number with a seat letter in $s array.

We insert a line break <br> after every 6 seats.

For that we check if modulo of 5 equals 0. This occurs when $j=5. Since $j starts with 0 we have 6 seats in a row before we insert a break.

Additionally, we check if $j is greater than 0 because 0 modulo 5 gives 0 and creates an extra break we do not want to have.

Output:

1A1B1C1D1E1F
2A2B2C2D2E2F
3A3B3C3D3E3F
4A4B4C4D4E4F
5A5B5C5D5E5F
6A6B6C6D6E6F
7A7B7C7D7E7F

$_GET and $_POST methods

Here you will learn how to use the request variables $_GET and $_POST. These variables provide you with different ways to transfer data from one web page to another. Let's look at the two methods, starting with GET. First, let's create a simple HTML form.

$_GET []

```
<html>
<head>
<title>Form Methods
</title>
</head>
```

```
 <body>
 <form method="get" action="actionpage.php">
 <p><input type="text" name="greeting"
size="15"></p>
 <p><input type="text" name="name" size="15"></p>
 <p><input type="submit" name="submit"
value="Salutation"></p>
 </form>
 </body>
 </html>
```

Save it as a form_methods.php file in the Apache htdocs/post folder created by you.

And now, we'll create a actionpage.php file for the Output: data transferred from the form.

```
<?
 echo $_GET ['greeting'];
 echo $_GET ['name'];
 echo "!";
 ?>
```

Save this file in the same directory as the form_methods.php file. This form looks like the following:

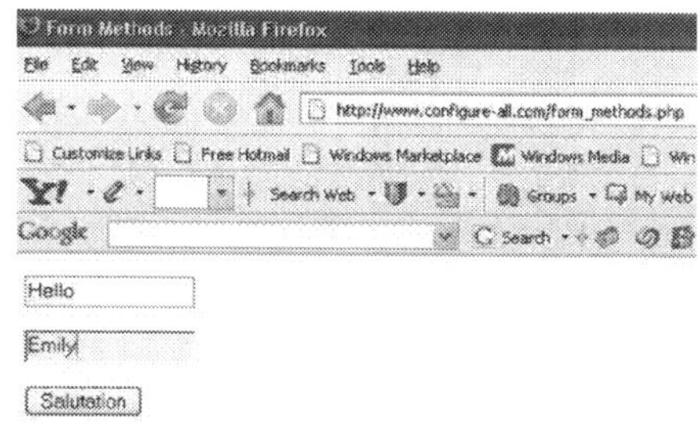

Figure 1. A simple HTML form

Let us enter a greeting and a name and click the Salutation button.

You can see that the data sent from a form with the GET method is displayed in the browser's address bar:

```
 http://localhost/post/formoutputpage.php? <=>
```

```
greeting=Hello&name=Emily&submit=Salutation
```

```
The Output web page displays Hello Emily!
```

$_POST []

Now let's use the POST method instead of the GET method. Edit form_method.php form.

```
<html>
<head>
<title>Form Methods</title>
</head>
<body>
<form method="post" action="formoutputpage.php">
<p><input type="text" name="greeting"
size="15"></p>
<p><input type="text" name="name" size="15"></p>
<p><input type="submit" name="submit"
value="Salutation"></p>
</form>
</body>
</html>
```

Edit formoutputpage.php file as follow:

```
<?
echo $_POST ['greeting'];
echo " ".$_POST ['name'];
echo "!";
?>
```

The browser address bar displays formoutputpage.php, but no data transferred using the POST method is visible, so the web page output remains the same:

Hello Emily!

You don't have to create a second page to read data submitted with form because it is possible to submit the form to the same page. To do this use super global $_SERVER ['PHP_SELF'].

```
<?php

$self=$_SERVER['PHP_SELF'];

$greeting="";
$name="";

If (isset ($_POST['greeting']))
$greeting=$_POST['greeting'];

If (isset ($_POST['name']))
$name=$_POST ['name'];

if (($name !="")&&($greeting!=""))
echo $greeting.' '.$name;

?>
<html>
<head>
<title>Form Methods
</title>
</head>
<body>
<?php
print('<form method="post"
action="'.$self.'">');
?>
<p><input type="text" name="greeting"
size="15"></p> 21
<p><input type="text" name="name" size="15"></p>
<p><input type="submit" name="submit"
value="Salutation"></p>
</form>
</body>
</html>
```

The htmlentities () function

The htmlentities () function is used for security reasons. It converts all characters to HTML entities.

For example, the '<' character will be converted to HTML '<'

If you add the ENT_QUOTES parameter, it will convert double quotes and single quotes to HTML entities.

```
<?php

$string='<a href="configure-all.com">Web
programming and design</a>';

echo htmlentities ($string, ENT_QUOTES). "<br>";

?>
```

Output (on the browser screen)

<a href="configure-all.com">Web programming and design</ a>.

If you view source you will see HTML characters:

<a href="configure-all.com">Web programming and design</ a>

The filter_var function (since PHP 5.2.0)

The filter_var function validates user input. Read more on the PHP.net website.

http:/ / us.php.net/ manual/ en/ filter.filters.validate.php

The example below validates the email address entered by a user.

```
<?php

function valid_email ($email) {

// filter_var returns false if email is invalid.

$email=filter_var ($email, FILTER_VALIDATE_EMAIL);

If (!$email)

echo "Email is invalid!";

else
```

```
echo $email;

}

valid_email ("master@configure-all.com");

echo "<br>";

valid_email ("masterconfigure-all.com");

?>
```

Output:
1. master@configure-all.com
2. "Email is not valid!"

When you pass an invalid email address to filter_var function (at the second echo) an empty string is returned.

Read about all exiting validate and sanitize filters on the PHP.net website.

Validate filters

FILTER_VALIDATE_BOOLEAN
FILTER_VALIDATE_EMAIL
FILTER_VALIDATE_FLOAT
FILTER_VALIDATE_INT
FILTER_VALIDATE_IP
FILTER_VALIDATE_REGEXP
FILTER_VALIDATE_URL

Sanitize filters

```
$email='maste" rconfi<> gur/e-all.com';
echo filter_var($email, FILTER_SANITIZE_EMAIL);
```

Output: master@configure-all.com

FILTER_SANITIZE_EMAIL
FILTER_SANITIZE_ENCODED
FILTER_SANITIZE_MAGIC_QUOTES
FILTER_SANITIZE_NUMBER_FLOAT

FILTER_SANITIZE_NUMBER_INT
FILTER_SANITIZE_SPECIAL_CHARS
FILTER_SANITIZE_FULL_SPECIAL_CHARS
FILTER_SANITIZE_STRING
FILTER_SANITIZE_STRIPPED
FILTER_SANITIZE_URL
FILTER_UNSAFE_RAW

Let us return to accessing the variables value submitted to the form using the POST method.

```
if (isset ($_POST ['lastname']))
$lastname= ($_POST ['lastname'];
```

If you didn't declare variables before the if statement, you will receive a notice displayed by PHP:

"Notice: Undefined variable name in C:\Apache2.2\htdocs\test\post.php on line 9"

The notice is displayed because the $lastname variable will be defined inside the if statement only. To have it defined anyplace on the page, you must declare it outside the if statement.

```
$lastname='';

if (isset ($_POST ['lastname']))

$lastname= ($_POST ['lastname'];
```

Now, no notice message will be displayed.

Pass $_GET Parameters to a Popup

Here I'll show you how to create a modeless popup to pass $_GET parameters from a parent page to the popup page. PHP and JavaScript are used to make this possible. First the JavaScript modelessparam function creates a modeless popup. Then you can pass parameters in the URL and read them in the popup page.

This is a script for the main page.

parent.php

```
<!DOCTYPE html>
<html lang="en">
<html>
<head> <title>Pass params to modeless
popup</TITLE>
<?php
$param1="Hello There!";
$param2="Hi World!";
?>
<script>
function modelessparam (url, width, height){

eval('window.open(url,"", "width='+ width + 'px,
<=>
height='+height+'px, resizable=1,
scrollbars=1")')
}
</script>
</head>
<body>
<p align="center"><input type="button"
name="greeting" <=>
value="Open Popup" <=>
onClick="javascript:modelessparam (<=>
'http://yourdomain/popup/popup.php?<=>
param1=<? echo $param1; ?> <=>
&param2=<? echo $param2; ?>',300, 200)"></p>
</form>
</body>
</html>
```

The bold code must be one line without breaks. The <=> is used as a carry-over sign only.

This is a script for a popup page:

popup.php

```
<!DOCTYPE html>
<html lang="en">
<head>
```

```
 <title>Popup with params from parent
window</title>
 <?
 if (isset ($_GET ['param1']))
 $param1 =$_GET['param1'];

 if (isset ($_GET ['param2']))
 $param2 =$_GET['param2'];
 ?>
 </head>

 <body>
 <?php
 print ('<p style="align:center; font-size:40px;
<=> color:#000;">'.$param1.'</p>');
 print ('<p style="align:center; font-size:50px;
<=>
 color: #000;">'.$param2.'</p>');
 ?>
 </body>
 </html>
```

Output: modeless window popup with text
Hello There!
Hi World!

$_COOKIE & $_SESSION

$_COOKIE []

Let us try to use the $_COOKIE [ ] global variable.

Edit form_methods.php by adding the following piece of code. The cookie code must be inserted before the HTML header. Otherwise, you will get an error!

The setcookie function will set the $pref variable to the $_COOKIE [] variable.

```
<?
 $pref="Mrs";
 setcookie ("prefix", $pref);
 ?>
 <html>
 <head>
 <title>Form Methods
 </title>
 </head>
 <body>
 <form method="post" action="formoutputpage.php">

 <p><input type="text" name="greeting"
size="15"></p>
 <p><input type="text" name="name" size="15"></p>
 <p><input type="submit" name="submit"
value="Salutation"></p>

 </form>
 </body>
 </html>
```

Edit the formoutputpage.php file like this:

```
 <?
 echo $_POST ['greeting'];
 echo " ".$_COOKIE ['prefix'];
 echo " ".$_POST ['name'];
 ?>
```

The output page displays:
Hello Mrs. Emily.

The setcookie function actually has many parameters; however, in this example, we will only use the following two: name and value.

On the PHP.net website you can find the whole description of any PHP function, including setcookie.

```
    "bool setcookie ( string $name [, string
$value [, int $expire = 0  [, string $path [,
string $domain  [, bool $secure = false  [, bool
$httponly = false ]]]]]] )"
```

If we had not used an expire parameter, our cookie would have expired when the browser closed. We did not use the path parameter, which means our cookie is accessible in the current directory only. For example, if your website page on which you set the cookie is in the root directory (public_html) and you have a subdirectory "public_html/upload" the cookie will not be accessible on the PHP page inside the upload directory. To make it accessible in all subdirectories, you should set path to "/" value. The path is the third parameter. If you use the third parameter you must also use the second parameter, "expire". You'll need to write the following:

setcookie ("prefix", $pref, 0, "/");

$_SESSION []

Let us try to use the session variable. The session code must be inserted before the HTML header. Otherwise, you will get an error! Edit form_methods.php file:

```
 <?
 session_start ();
 $_SESSION ['title'] ="Dr.";
 setcookie ("prefix", $pref, 0, "/");
 ?>
 <html>
 <head>
 <title>Form Methods
 </title>
 </head>
 <body>
 <form method="post" action="formoutputpage.php">
 <p><input type="text" name="greeting"
 size="15"></p>
 <p><input type="text" name="name" size="15"></p>
 <p><input type="submit" name="submit"
value="Salutation"></p>
 </form>
 </body>
```

```
</html>
```

Edit formoutputpage.php file. The session_start () function starts the session. It must be used each time you assign value to the $_SESSION variable or read value from the $_SESSION variable.

```
<?
session_start ();
echo $_POST ['greeting'];
echo " ".$_SESSION ['title'];
echo " ".$_COOKIE ['prefix'];
echo " ".$_POST ['name'];
?>
```

The output page will display:
Hello Dr. Mrs. Emily

You can transfer data from one page to another via link. Edit form_methods.php file. Data sent by link is transferred by the GET method. It can be read from the $_GET [] variable.

With a link you can pass as many parameters as you want. The first parameter starts following a question mark character, after which an ampersand character is placed before each parameter as in the following example:

page.php?param1=value1¶m2=value2¶m3=value3 and so on.

HTTP protocol does not specify any maximum URL length. That would depend on the browser.

```
<?
session_start ();
$_SESSION ['title'] ="Dr.";
setcookie ("prefix","Mrs");
?>
<html>
<head>
<title>Form Methods
</title>
</head>
<body>
<form method="post" action="formoutputpage.php">
```

```
 <p><input type="text" name="greeting"
size="15"></p>
 <p><input type="text" name="name" size="15"></p>
 <p><input type="submit" name="submit"
value="Salutation"></p>

 </form>
 <?
 $greeting="Good morning"
 $person="Michael";
 print ('<p><a href="link_output.php?
 greeting='.$greeting.'&person='.$person.'">Link
output</a>');
 ?>
 </body></html>
```

When hovering your mouse over the link, $_GET variables are displayed on the browser task bar.

Figure 2. Task bar with the URL.

Create link_output.php file.

```
<?

$greeting=$_GET['greeting'];

$person=$_GET['person'];

echo $greeting." ".$person."!";

?>
```

Click the link on the form_methods.php page and you will get the output:

Good morning Michael!

To use the $_REQUEST [] variable that contains contents of $_GET, $_POST and $_COOKIE variables, edit formoutputpage.php as follows:

```
<?
session_start ();
echo $_REQUEST ['greeting'];
echo " ".$_SESSION ['title'];
echo " ".$_REQUEST ['prefix'];
echo " ".$_REQUEST ['name'];
?>
```

Fill in the form and submit. Output will be the same: Hello Dr. Mrs. Emily!

Also, you can insert statement <b> import_request_variables ("pgc",""); </b> and use the form input field names to access $_GET [], $_POST [] and $_COOKIE []. However, I would strongly recommend that the <b> import request variables</b> statement not be used due to security reasons.

Edit the formoutputpage.php file as follows:

```
<?
import_request_variables ("pgc","");

session_start ();

echo $greeting;
echo " ".$_SESSION ['title'];
echo " ".$prefix;
echo " ".$name;
?>
```

Submit the form again and you will get the same output: Hello Dr. Mrs. Emily!

Click the link on the form and you will get output: Good morning Michael!

Useful PHP date and time functions.

Use the PHP date function to get today's date.

It has the format parameter that allows date creation in various formats. The US date format begins with the month followed by the day and then the year: For example, "02/14/2023" is Valentine's Day.

In Europe, the date format is different. First is noted the day, then the month, and then the year.

For example, Valentine's Day would be written "14/02/2023".

When saving a date in a MySQL database, it should have the following format: Year, dash, month, dash and day. For MySQL, Valentine's Day is "2023-02-14". When saving the date in an Oracle database, the format is "14-FEB-23".

When we run the code on Valentine Day, we get the following date formats:

```
$today1=date('m-d-y');
echo "today1=".$today1."<br>";
```

Output: today1=02-14-23

Small letters in date format function mean numeric day, month or year.

Capital M means 3 letters month format.

Capital D means day of the week

Capital Y means 4 digits year.

```
$today2=date ('m-d-Y');
echo "today2=".$today2."<br>";
```

Output: today2=02-14-2023

```
$today3=date ('M-d-Y');
echo "today3=".$today3."<br>";
```

Output: today3=Feb-14-2023

```
$today4=date ('M-D-Y');
```

```
echo "today4=".$today4."<br>";
```

Output: today4=Feb-Tue-20223

We can use the strtotime function to change the format of any date.

The strtotime function converts a string data type to a date data type according to the format parameter of the date function.

$US_date=date ('m/d/Y', strtotime ('February 14, 2023));

```
echo "US_date=".$US_date."<br>";
```

Output: US_date=02/14/2023

```
$europe_date=date ('d/m/Y', strtotime ('February 14,2023));
echo "Output: europe_date=".$europe_date."<br>";
```

Output: europe_date=14/02/2023

```
$mysql_date=date ('Y-m-d', strtotime ('February
14,2023));
echo "Output: mysql_date=".$mysql_date."<br>";
```

Output: mysql_date=2023-02-14

```
$oracle_date=date ("d-M-y", strtotime ('February
14,2023));
echo "Output: oracle date= $oracle_date."<br>";
```

Output: oracle date=14-Feb-23

mktime function returns the number of seconds between the Unix epoch (January 1 1970 00:00:00 GMT) and the time specified.

The following displays the date 6 months ago:

```
$monthago6 = date ("d-M-y", mktime (0, 0, 0, date
("m")-6,
date ("d"), date ("Y")));
```

```
echo "month6ago=". $monthago6."<br>";
```

Output: month6ago=15-NOV-17 if the code run on 05/15/17

```
$monthago6 = date ("m/d/Y", mktime (0, 0, 0, date
("m")-6,
date ("d"), date ("Y")));
echo "month6ago=". $monthago6."<br>";
```

Output: month6ago=11/15/2017

```
$yesterday = date ("m/d/y", mktime (0, 0, 0, date
("m"),
date ("d")-1, date ("Y")));
echo "yesterday=". $yesterday."<br>";
```

Output: yesterday=05/14/17

```
$tomorrow = date ("m/d/y", mktime (0, 0, 0, date
("m"),
date ("d")+1, date ("Y")));
echo "tomorrow=". $tomorrow."<br>";
```

Output: tomorrow=05/16/17

```
$lastyear= date ("m/d/y", mktime (0, 0, 0, date
("m"), date ("d"), date ("Y")-1));
echo "lastyear=". $lastyear."<br>";
```

Output: lastyear =05/15/16

```
$nextyear= date ("m/d/y", mktime (0, 0, 0, date
("m"), date ("d"), date ("Y")+1));
echo "nextyear=". $nextyear."<br>";
```

Output: nextyear=05/15/23

Working with files

To open a file with PHP you can use the fopen () function. It requires a path to a file with a file name and a mode string. In the notepad type the following:

"How to open file in PHP? Use fopen function."

Save file as "C:\\Apache2.2\htdocs\test\myfile.txt". First, we will use the fgetc () function.

The fgetc function gets a character from the file pointer.

```
$fh=fopen ("myfile.txt","r");
$fh=fopen ('http://127.0.0.1/test/myfile.php',
'r');
   while(!feof
 ($fh)) {
  $char = fgetc ($fh);
  print $char;
  }

  fclose ($fh);
```

Output: How to open file in PHP? Use the fopen function.

The fgets function gets a line from the file pointer.

```
 $fp=fopen('http://127.0.0.1/test/myfile.txt',
'r');

  while  ($line = fgets  ($fp)) {
  echo $line."<br>";
  }

  fclose ($fp);
```

Output:

How to open file in PHP Use the fopen function.

Displaying a Record from a csv File

Here you will learn how to read a csv file and display its fields' values on a web page.

A complete PHP source code is provided.

Download the filetoread.csv http://www.learn-coding.today/phpbook/filetoread.csv.txt file with tab delimited fields. For simplicity the file has only six fields and three records.

Part	number	Product	Company	link	Price
part1	1	PC	HP	http://www.domain.com	$29.99
part2	2	PC	DELL	http://www.domain.com	$39.99
part3	3	PC	HP	http://www.domain.com	$49.99

Create a datafeed directory in your website root directory and save the filetoread.csv file to the datafeed directory. Look at the file records.

The PHP file with source code, which reads the csv file, can be downloaded from http://www.learn-coding.today/phpbook/readcsv.txt

readscv.php

```
<?php

 //create table with header and column names
 print ('<table align="center" width="800">');
 print ('<tr><td colspan="6">
Computer electronics</td></tr>');
  print ('<tr><td>Part</td><td> number</td>
  <td>Product</td><td>Company</td>
 <td>Link</td><td>Price</td></tr>');

//declare variable to count records
$rowcount = 0;

//get path to file if file located in datafeed
//folder
$path_to_file="datafeed/filetoread.csv";

//open file for reading "r"

$handle = fopen ($path_to_file, "r");

//read file line by line.
//1000 is string length, " " is delimiter
```

```
while(($record = fgetcsv($handle, 1000, " "))!==
FALSE)
{// read number of fields in one record

 $numfields = count ($record);

   /*Display all fields for debugging to know
  which data is in which field. In the real scv
  datafeed file of an affiliated program are a
  lot of stored data fields you don't need. By
  using the output below, you can see what
  fields to select to create an advertisement on
  your web page*/
  /*comment code below in production version*/

   for ($i=0; $i< $numfields; $i++)
   {
   echo $i.":". $record [$i]."<br>";
 }

   /* end debugging part */
 //read field values in variable

 $part=$record [0];
 $number=$record [1];
 $product=$record [2];
 $company=$record [3];
 $clicklink=$record [4];
 $price=$record [5];

/* skip the first record since it has field
headers only */

   if ($rowcount > 0) {
 /* if record has link to item display it in the
table row */

   if ($record [3] !="") {
  print ('<tr><td>'. $part.'</td><td>'. $number.
  '</td><td>'. $product.'</td><td>'. $company.
  '</td><td><a href="' .$clicklink.'">'.
  $product. '</a></td><td>'.
  $price.'</td></tr>');
```

```
        }
}

   $rowcount++;
}

   fclose ($handle);
   print('</table>');
?>
```

Download the readcsv.txt file and save it as .php file in your web site root directory.
Download the filetoread.csv file with tab delimited fields.
Remove txt extension after downloading files.
Include the file with code in the web page you want to display records from the csv file.

```
<?
include ('readscv.php');
?>
```

We are done. To read all PHP function related to a file system visit the PHP.net site:
http://us3.php.net/manual/en/book.filesystem.php

Upload File PHP code example

You can take this PHP code example and modify it to for your needs.
To prevent overwriting files uploaded earlier, I use current date and time for a new file name.
The PHP code example is comprised of two PHP files. The first PHP file represents a form that allows a user to browse a local file system, select a file for uploading, and submitting the form. I named it "upload_file.php". The second PHP file is an action template that executes uploading the selected file. I named it "act_upload_file.php".
On my Windows PC, I created a folder "uploadfile" inside the htdocs folder and placed both files inside the uploadfile folder. Besides, I created "upload" folder inside the "uploadfile" folder.

On the hosting web server, you have to make sure that the user has written permission for the "upload" folder. However, if you use the following code example on your local Windows PC, there will be no need for concern about that.
upload_file.php

```
 <?php
print ('<html>');
print ('<head><title>');
print ('Upload File Example</title>');
print ('</head>');
print ('<body>');
print ('<form name="myform" ENCTYPE ="multipart/
form-data" method="post"
action="act_upload_file.php">');
print ('<table align="center" width="80%">');
print ('<tr><th align="center">Upload File
Example</th></tr>');
print ('<INPUT TYPE="hidden" name="MAX_FILE_SIZE"
value="1000000">');
print ('<tr><td align="center">Upload File:
<INPUT NAME="uploaded_file" TYPE="file"></td>
</tr>');
print ('<tr><td> </td></tr>');
print ('<tr><td align="center" >
<input type="submit" name="submit"
value="Upload"> </td></tr>');
 print ('</table></form>');
 print ('<body></html>');
 ?>
```

The form data encoding type, enctype must be "multipart/form-data"
The MAX_FILE_SIZE hidden field must precede the file input field. The MAX_FILE_SIZE is measured in bytes. To convert a 1MB image to kilobytes, multiply by 1024 and to further convert kilobytes to bytes, again, multiply by 1024, i.e., 1 * 1024^2 =1048576 bytes.
If MAX_FILE_SIZE="1000000" you can upload images up to 0.95MB

When a user selects a file to upload and clicks the Upload button, the form will send an $_FILES array like the following:
Array([uploaded_file] => Array ([name] => bird.jpg
[type] => image/jpeg [tmp_name] =>
C:\Windows\Temp\phpBCDC.tmp
[error] => 0 [size] => 56869))
Uploaded_file is the name of the file field, bird.jpg is the original file name, type is the type of the uploaded file, tmp_name is a new temporary file path and name, and its size is the size of the uploaded file in bytes.
act_upload_file.php

```
<?php
 $uploaded=0;
 $ext="";
 //generate unique file name using time:
 $newfilename= md5 (rand () * time ());
 //do we have a file?
 if ((!empty ($_FILES["uploaded_file"])) &&
   ($_FILES ['uploaded_file']['error'] == 0)){
 $filename =strtolower(basename($_FILES
['uploaded_file']
   ['name']));
 $ext = substr($filename, strrpos($filename, '.')
+ 1);
 if ((($ext == "jpg")||($ext == "JPG")) &&
   ($_FILES ["uploaded_file"] ["size"] < 500000)&&
   (($_FILES ["uploaded_file"] ["type"] ==
"image/jpeg")||
   ($_FILES ["uploaded_file"] ["type"] ==
"image/pjpeg"))){

 //Determine the path to which we want to save
this file
 $ext=".". $ext;
 $newname=dirname (__FILE__).'/upload/'.
$newfilename.$ext;

 if((move_uploaded_file ($_FILES
['uploaded_file']
   ['tmp_name'], $newname))) {
 echo "File uploaded successfully!";
```

```
$uploaded=1;
} else {
echo "Error!";
print ('<p><a
href="upload_file.php?">Back</a></p>');
}
} else {
echo "Error: Only .jpg files is allowed less
than 950Kb";
print ('<p><a
href="upload_file.php">Back</a></p>');
}
} else {
echo "Error! File is not uploaded!";
print ('<p><a
href="upload_file.php">Back</a></p>');
}
?>
```

If you wish to limit image width and height, use the getimagesize function:

list ($width, $height, $type, $attr) = getimagesize ($_FILES ['uploaded_file'] ['tmp_name']);

$width and $height variables give you the image size.

Try to modify the PHP code example. Provide user an input field for a new file name. Think about how to check if this file already exists on the server and alert the user.

Draw and Display Images

To use PHP image functions, uncomment the extension=php_gd2.dll line in the PHP.INI file.

Find the PHP.INI file in both the "C:\PHP" directory and "C:\windows\System32\" directory.

Open the php.ini file, scroll down to the Windows Extensions and delete the ";" character in front of gd2.dll as shown below:

```
PHP.INI
;extension=php_bz2.dll
;extension=php_curl.dll
;extension=php_dba.dll
;extension=php_dbase.dll
```

```
;extension=php_fdf.dll
extension=php_gd2.dll
;extension=php_gettext.dll
;extension=php_gmp.dll
;extension=php_ifx.dll
;extension=php_imap.dll
;extension=php_interbase.dll
;extension=php_ldap.dll
;extension=php_mbstring.dll
;extension=php_exif.dll
;extension=php_mcrypt.dll
;extension=php_mhash.dll
;extension=php_mime_magic.dll
;extension=php_ming.dll
;extension=php_msql.dll
;extension=php_mssql.dll
extension=php_mysql.dll
extension=php_mysqli.dll
;extension=php_oci8.dll
;extension=php_openssl.dll
extension=php_pdo.dll
;extension=php_pdo_firebird.dll
;extension=php_pdo_mssql.dll
extension=php_pdo_mysql.dll
;extension=php_pdo_oci.dll
;extension=php_pdo_oci8.dll
;extension=php_pdo_odbc.dll
;extension=php_pdo_pgsql.dll
;extension=php_pdo_sqlite.dll
;extension=php_pgsql.dll
;extension=php_pspell.dll
;extension=php_shmop.dll
;extension=php_snmp.dll
;extension=php_soap.dll
;extension=php_sockets.dll
;extension=php_sqlite.dll
;extension=php_sybase_ct.dll
;extension=php_tidy.dll
;extension=php_xmlrpc.dll
```

;extension=php_xsl.dll
;extension=php_zip.dll

Open notepad or textpad and write a PHP code:

Draw a Rectangle

```
<?php
//Create a blank image
$img=imagecreatetruecolor(350, 200);
//allocate colors
$pink = imagecolorallocate($img, 255, 105, 180);
$green = imagecolorallocate($img, 000, 255, 255);
//draw empty rectangle
imagerectangle($img, 0, 0, 348, 198, $pink);
//fill rectangle with the allocated color
imagefilledrectangle($img, 10, 10, 340, 190,
$green);
header('Content-type: image/jpeg');
//display image
 imagejpeg($img);
 imagedestroy($img);
?>
```

Run the script and a Rectangle is displayed.

Figure 3. The rectangle.

Color Codes in RGB

RGB stands for Red Green Blue—the three basic colors.
255, 0, 0 is Red
0, 255, 0 is Green
0, 0, 255 is Blue
255, 255, 255 is while
0,0,0 is Black
Color codes may be represented by hexadecimal numbers.
FF0000 is Red
00FF00 is Green
0000FF is Blue

Draw a Graph

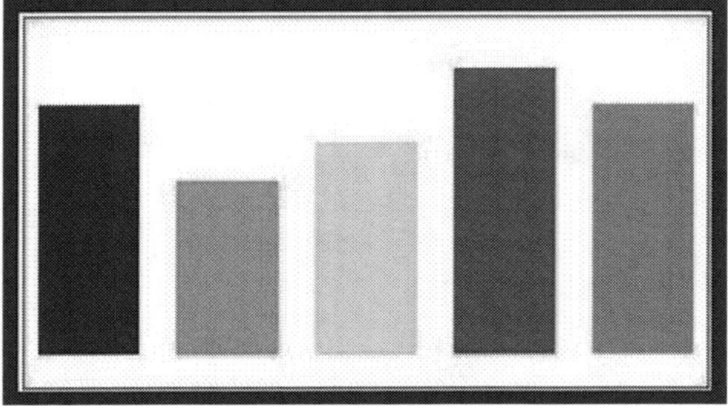

Figure 4. The graph.

```
<?php
 // // Create a blank image
 $img=imagecreatetruecolor(350, 200);

 //allocate colors for main rectangle and graphs
 $pink = imagecolorallocate($img, 255, 105, 180);
 $green = imagecolorallocate($img, 000, 255,
100);
 $white = imagecolorallocate($img, 255, 255,
255);
 $red = imagecolorallocate($img, 255, 0, 0);
 $yellow = imagecolorallocate($img, 240, 255, 0);
 $blue = imagecolorallocate($img, 0, 0, 255);
```

```
 //create main white filled rectangle for graph
 imagefilledrectangle($img, 0, 0, 350, 200,
$white);
 //create red empty rectangle
 imagerectangle($img, 2, 2, 348, 198, $red);

 //fill rectangles for each graph
 imagefilledrectangle($img, 10, 50, 60, 180,
$blue);
 imagefilledrectangle($img, 80, 90, 130, 180,
$green);
 imagefilledrectangle($img, 150, 70, 200, 180,
$yellow);
 imagefilledrectangle($img, 220, 30, 270, 180,
$red);
 imagefilledrectangle($img, 290, 50, 340, 180,
$pink);

 header('Content-type: image/jpeg');

 //display image
 imagejpeg ($img);
 imagedestroy ($img);
 ?>
```

Draw a Polygon

```
<?php
 // Create a blank image
 $image = imagecreatetruecolor (400, 300);
 $arraybg=array (10,50, 130,20, 350,100, 300,200,
150,230,30,150);
$array=array(15,55,130,25,340,105,290,195,150,220
,
  35,145);
 // Allocate a color for the polygon and
//background polygon
 $yellow = imagecolorallocate($image,240,255,0);
 $blue = imagecolorallocate ($image, 0, 0, 255);
 // fill the polygon
 imagefilledpolygon($image,$arraybg,6,$yellow);
```

```
// Draw the polygon
imagepolygon ($image, $array, 6, $blue);

// Output the picture to the browser
header('Content-type: image/png');

imagepng($image);
imagedestroy($image);
?>
```

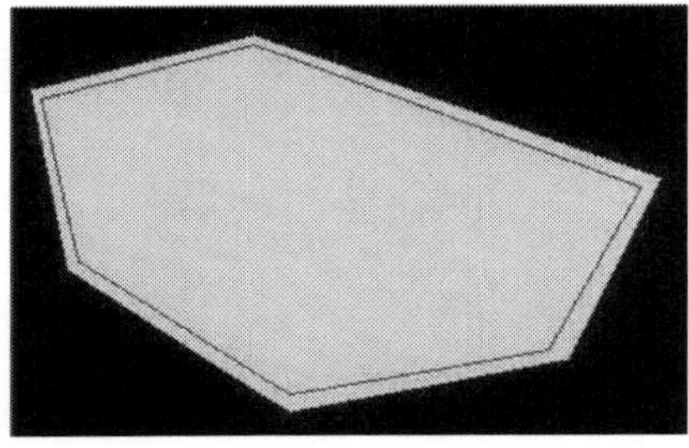

Figure 5. A polygon.

The Pie Graph

To draw a pie graph, we will use the imagearc () function.

```
bool imagearc (resource $image, int $cx, int $cy,
int $width, int $height, int $start, int $end,
int $color )
```

Visit the PHP.net web site for details:
http://us.php.net/manual/en/function.imagearc.php

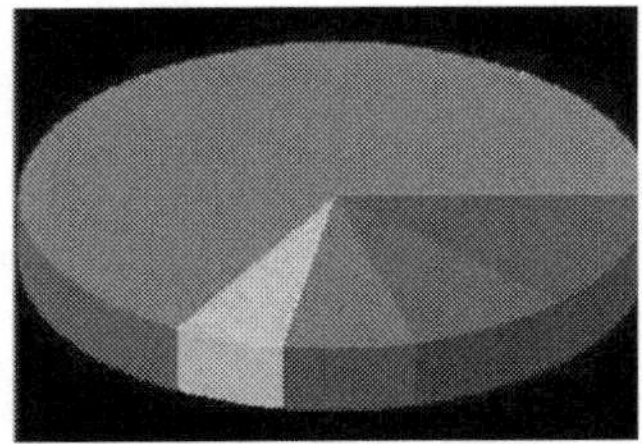

Figure 6. The pie graph.

```
<?php
// create image
$img = imagecreatetruecolor (300, 300);
// allocate some light and dark color pairs
$pink = imagecolorallocate ($img, 255, 51, 102);
$darkpink = imagecolorallocate ($img,184, 0, 46);
$red=imagecolorallocate ($img, 184,138, 0);
$darkred=imagecolorallocate ($img, 184, 46, 0);
$yellow=imagecolorallocate ($img, 204, 255, 51);
$darkyellow=imagecolorallocate ($img,255,204,51);
$blue = imagecolorallocate ($img, 51, 102, 255);
$darkblue = imagecolorallocate ($img, 0,61, 245);
$green = imagecolorallocate ($img, 0, 240, 0);
$darkgreen = imagecolorallocate ($img, 0,179,0);

 // make the 3D effect
 for($i = 180; $i > 150; $i--) {
 imagefilledarc($img, 150, $i, 300, 150, 0, 45,
$darkblue, IMG_ARC_PIE);
 imagefilledarc ($img, 150, $i, 300, 150, 45, 75,
$darkpink, IMG_ARC_PIE);
 imagefilledarc ($img, 150, $i, 300, 150, 75,
100, $darkred, IMG_ARC_PIE);
imagefilledarc($img, 150, $i, 300, 150, 100, 120,
$darkyellow, IMG_ARC_PIE);
imagefilledarc ($img, 150, $i, 300, 150, 120,
360, $darkgreen, IMG_ARC_PIE);
}
imagefilledarc ($img, 150, 150, 300, 150, 0, 45,
$blue, IMG_ARC_PIE);
imagefilledarc ($img, 150, 150, 300, 150, 45, 75,
$pink, IMG_ARC_PIE);
imagefilledarc ($img, 150, 150, 300, 150, 75,
100, $red, IMG_ARC_PIE);
imagefilledarc ($img, 150, 150, 300, 150, 100,
120, $yellow, IMG_ARC_PIE);
 imagefilledarc ($img, 150, 150, 300, 150, 120,
 360, $green, IMG_ARC_PIE);
 // flush image
 header ('Content-type: image/png');
 imagepng ($img);
 imagedestroy ($img);
```

```
?>
```

Draw a Caption

You can draw a caption on your picture, using the imagestring () function:

```
<?php
$im=imagecreatefromjpeg('images/geese.jpg');
$textcolor=imagecolorallocate($im,255,255,255);
// Write the string at the bottom
imagestring($im,5,150,301,'Wild Geese in a
Pond!', $textcolor);
// Output the image
header ('Content-type: image/png');
imagepng ($im);
imagedestroy ($im);
?>
```

Figure 7. The Caption

The picture with the caption will be displayed. The code is easy to understand.

1. You get the path to the image file.
2. Create the image using the imagecreatefromjpeg function (for jpg image file).

3. Set mime type in your header so your browser will know what kind of data will be sent to it.

4. Display the image in your browser using the imagejpeg function. In addition, the imagejpeg function has two other arguments. It can output the image in a file:

```
imagejpeg ($image, "newfile.jpg", 50);
```

The third argument is image quality. If you enter a file name a jpg file will be created; however, the browser will not display the image.

This is a caption with custom fonts and an angle.

```
<?php
$im=imagecreatefromjpeg('images/DSC02646.jpg');
$textcolor = imagecolorallocate($im, 255, 255,
255);
$font ='11825.ttf';
$font_size = 30;
$left=200;
$top=180;
$angle=20;
imagettftext($im, $font_size, $angle, $left,
$top, $textcolor, $font, "WINDOW ROCK AZ");
// Output the image
header('Content-type: image/png');
imagepng($im);
//imagedestroy($im);
?>
```

Figure 8. A caption with the custom fonts.

To display a date on the image, get the image height; allocate a color, display a caption text with font 5 and color white, and then size it 100 pixels from the left and 50 from the bottom.

```
<?php
 $imagepath="phpimages/dog.jpg";
 $image=imagecreatefromjpeg ($imagepath);
 // get image height
 $imgheight=imagesy($image);

 //allocate color for image caption (white)
$color=imagecolorallocate ($image, 255, 255,
255);

 //Add text to the image bottom
 imagestring ($image, 5, 100, $imgheight-50, "May
2012", $color);

 header ('Content-Type: image/jpeg');
 imagejpeg ($image);
 ?>
```

The problem with this code is that you cannot display any text on the page because the mime type is set for image/jpeg. If you want to display the image on the page with the text, use the image.php file as your source for the img src tag.

Download all php code examples with drawings or images.

www.learn-coding.today/phpbook/image.zip

Display images from a directory

I will show you how I display an images gallery on my web page. First, I created a main images directory in my root directory. Then I created a directory for thumbnail images. I used a PHP script to resize each main image and create thumbnails. Then I saved each image in the thumbnail images directory with the same name as the main image. Download the source code:

www.learn-coding.today/phpbook/image.zip

Then I displayed all the thumbnail images on one page in a table. Each thumbnail image has a link to the main image.

When the user clicks a thumbnail, a corresponding single main image is displayed on the next page.

Resize images to create thumbnails

```
<?php

function create_thumb($original_image,
$thumb_width, $thumb_image, $thumbdir,
$orig_image_dir)
{
$max_width=$thumb_width;

//Check if GD extension is loaded
if (!extension_loaded('gd'))
{
trigger_error("gd is not loaded",
E_USER_WARNING);
return false;
}

//Get Image size info
list($width_orig, $height_orig, $image type) =
getimagesize($orig_image_dir."/".$original_image)
;

$image_orig =
imagecreatefromjpeg($orig_image_dir.'/'.$original
_image);

//calculate the height/width ratio
$h_to_w_ratio = (float) $height_orig /
$width_orig;

//calulate the thumbnail width based on the
height
$thumb_height = round($thumb_width *
$h_to_w_ratio);

while($thumb_height>$max_width)
{
$thumb_width-=10;
```

```
$thumb_height = round($thumb_width *
$h_to_w_ratio);
}

$newImg = imagecreatetruecolor($thumb_width,
$thumb_height);

imagecopyresampled($newImg, $image_orig, 0, 0, 0,
0, $thumb_width, $thumb_height, $width_orig,
$height_orig);

//Generate the file, and rename it to
$thumb_image
imagejpeg($newImg, $thumbdir."/".$thumb_image);

return $thumb_image;
}?>
```

If you have main images in your images directory and you want to create a thumbnail image in the thumb directory, place directory names in the function arguments.

```
<?php

$files=array ();
$count=0;
$files=scandir (dirname (__FILE__)."/images/");
$count=count ($files);

for ($i=2; $i < $count; $i++) {
echo create_thumb($files[$i], 170,
$files[$i],'thumb', 'images');
 }
 ?>
```

Display thumbnails

Now when you have created thumbnail images in the thumb directory, you may display these images on your web page. Again, as you can see below, I used the scandir function to get image names:

```
<?php

 $files=array ();
 $images=array ();
 $count=0;

 $files=scandir(dirname(__FILE__)."/".
$thumb."/");

 $count=sizeof($files);

 //two first file name are not valid images for
//some reason, and you have to skip them.

 for ($i=0; $i<$count; $i++) {

 if ($i >1)
 $images[]=$files [$i];
 }
 $count=sizeof($images);
 print('<table><tr>');
  for ($i=0; $i<$count; $i++) {
 //pass image name to the main image directory to
   //display large image on the next page.

 print ('<td><a href="largeimage.php?path='.
 $orig_image_dir.'/'.$images [$i].'">
 <img src="'.$thumb.'/'.$images[$i].'"></a>
</td>');

 if (($i+1) % 6==0)
 print ('</tr><tr>');
 }
 print ('</tr></table>');
 ?>
```

Display large image

On the largeimage.php page display the main image:

```
<?php
 $imagefile="";
 if (isset ($_GET ['path']))
 $imagefile=$_GET['path'];
 print('<table><tr><td>');
 print ('<img src="'.$imagefile.'" width="593"
 alt="an image caption"/>');
 print ('</td></tr></table>');
 ?>
```

To see what it looks like on one of my sites, click on the following link:

http://sergeyskudaev.com/images.php

How to run PHP script in the background

Sometimes, your PHP script performs a task that requires time. If it takes more than a minute, the browser may display 504 gateway timeout. If you do not need to display to the user any message while the task is performed, you can run your PHP script in the background without a browser.
Using a batch file is one way to run a PHP script in the background. Let's use a simple PHP script that creates an image of the sun, a yellow circle on a blue background. See Figure 9.

Figure 9. The Sun.

If the image file is created, it will prove that our script is executed.

Create a batch file with the following code. This example of a batch file is for Windows PC

```
@echo off
REM this command runs a PHP script.
start "run php", "C:\php\php.exe" -f C:\phpprojects\sun.php 500
500
```

The @echo off command prevents displaying the contents of the batch file on the command prompt. If you want to display it, change @echo off to @echo on. The REM command allows entering a line of comments in the batch file. "c:\php\php.exe" is a path to the PHP executable. The "C:\phpprojects\sun.php" is a path to your PHP file.
500 and 500 are two parameters for the image width and height. These parameters can be read from the $argv array in the PHP script.
You can visit this command line reference website: https://ss64.com/ if you want to learn more about the command prompt.
Here is our PHP file to create the sun image.
Sun.php

```
<?php
//Read parameters from $argv array.
$height=$argv[1];
$width=$argv[2];
//Create a blank image.
$img=imagecreatetruecolor ($width, $height);
//allocate colors.
$lightblue = imagecolorallocate($img, 0, 195,
255);
$yellow = imagecolorallocate($img, 255, 255, 0);
//Create a filled blue rectangle.
imagefilledrectangle($img, 0, 0, $width, $height,
$lightblue );
//Create a filled yellow circle.
imagefilledellipse($img, $width/2, $height/2,
$width/2, $height/2, $yellow);
//Create the image jpg file.
imagejpeg($img,'images/sun.jpg', 100);
//display image in the browser
```

```
header('Content-type: image/jpeg');
imagejpeg($img);
imagedestroy($img);
?>
```

You can run the sun.php file in a browser first to make sure that it works. The image file will be created, and the image will be displayed in the browser. Delete the image. Then go to the command prompt and run the batch file.
In my case, my batch file and my sun.php file are located in the C:\phpprojects directory. My php.exe file is located in the C:\php directory. Go to phpprojects directory, type run.bat, and press enter. The batch file will be executed, and the PHP script will create the image in the C:\phpprojects/images directory. Here is my command prompt screenshot.

```
Microsoft Windows [Version 10.0.19044.2846]
(c) Microsoft Corporation. All rights reserved.

C:\Users\Owner>cd..

C:\Users>cd..

C:\>cd phpprojects

C:\phpprojects>run.bat

C:\phpprojects>
```

You can execute your PHP script with the PHP file you run in the browser. To execute a PHP script in the background with a PHP, create the following PHP file.

run_to_argv.php:

```
<?php
exec("php -f arc_pie.php 255 0 0");
?>
```

In this case, as an example of a PHP script, we will use the arc_pie.php file, which creates a pie diagram. The run_to_argv.php file includes the exec built-in PHP function. This function has one argument – a command string. This string includes php command -f and the path to the php file. The 255 255 0 are three parameters for RGB image color. They can be read from $argv array in the called PHP file.

arc_pie.php

```
$red=$argv[1];

$green=$argv[2];

$blue=$argv[3];

//if no parameters are entered, use the default.
if($red=="")
$red=255;
if($green=="")
$green=255;
if($blue=="")
$blue=0;

$width=3000;
$height=3000;

//Create a blank image
$img=imagecreatetruecolor ($width, $height);

//allocate colors
$color = imagecolorallocate($img, $red, $green,
$blue);
$background = imagecolorallocate($img, 0, 125,
255);

//draw a filled rectangle
imagefilledrectangle($img, 0, 0, $width, $height,
$background);

//draw a filled arc

imagefilledarc(
    $img,         //GdImage
    $width/2,     //center_x
    $height/2,     //center_y
    $width-20,     //width
    $height-20,     //height
```

```
    0,            //start_angle 3 o'clock
    270,          //end_angle 12 o'clock
    $color,       //color
     IMG_ARC_PIE  //style
);
imagejpeg($img, 'images/arc_pie.jpg',90);
header('Content-type: image/jpeg');
//display image
imagejpeg($img);
imagedestroy($img);
?>
```

Run the arc_pie.php file in the browser to make sure it does not have errors. The pie diagram image will be created and displayed in the browser. Delete the image.
Then run the run_to_argv.php file in the browser or command prompt. In both cases, the pie diagram image will be created.
There is a different way to pass parameters to a PHP file. In that case, the parameters are stored in the $_GET array.
run_to_get.php:

```
<?php
exec("php-cgi -f arc_pie.php red=0 green=0
blue=255");
?>
```

arc_pie.php:

```
<?php
$red="";
$green="";
$blue="";

if($red=="")
$red=$argv[1];
if($green=="")
$green=$argv[2];
if($blue=="")
$blue=$argv[3];

// If $argv is empty read  $_GET
if($red=="")
$red=$_GET['red'];
```

```
if($green=="")

$green=$_GET['green'];

if($blue=="")

$blue=$_GET['blue'];


//if no parameters are entered, use the default.
if($red=="")
$red=255;
if($green=="")
$green=255;
if($blue=="")
$blue=0;

$width=3000;
$height=3000;

//Create a blank image
$img=imagecreatetruecolor ($width, $height);

//allocate colors
$color = imagecolorallocate($img, $red, $green,
$blue);
$bgrndcolor = imagecolorallocate($img, 0, 125,
255);

//draw a filled rectangle
imagefilledrectangle($img, 0, 0, $width, $height,
$bgrndcolor);

//draw a filled arc

imagefilledarc(
    $img,          //GdImage
    $width/2,      //center_x
    $height/2,      //center_y
    $width-20,      //width
    $height-20,      //height
    0,             //start_angle 3 o'clock
    270,           //end_angle 12 o'clock
    $color,        //color
     IMG_ARC_PIE  //style
```

```
);
imagejpeg($img, 'images/arc_pie.jpg',90);
header('Content-type: image/jpeg');
//display image
imagejpeg($img);
imagedestroy($img);
?>
```

When you run the run_to_argv.php, the output is a red arc because we passed RGB = 255, 0, 0. See Figure 110

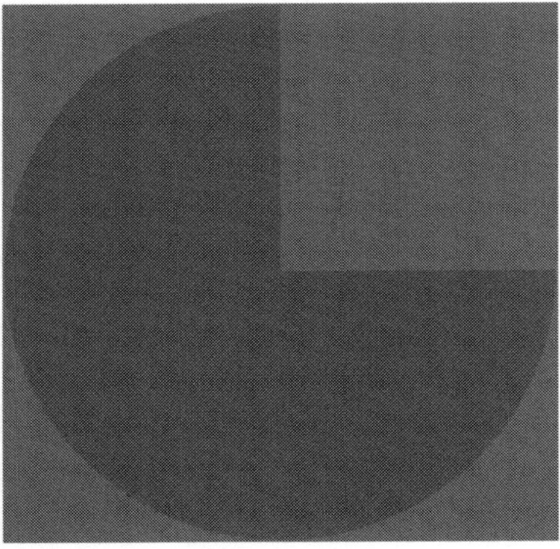

Figure 10. A red arc. RGB=255, 0, 0

When you run ***run_to_get.php***, the output is a dark blue arc because we passed RGB = 0, 0, 255. See Figure 11.

Figure 11. A dark blue arc. RGB=0, 0, 255

If no parameters are passed, the default parameters are used, and the yellow arc is displayed.

Object Oriented Programming

In this tutorial you will learn about Object Oriented Programming in PHP. I will not include any theory or history of Object Oriented Programming here. You can find it on Wikipedia.

I will give you a simple code example in procedural style to help you understand the concept.

Then we'll use the same code example with functions. And finally, we'll take the same example using a class (OOP approach).

Let us create a simple form that will allow us to enter two numbers and a simple PHP code that will calculate the sum, difference between, multiplication, and division of the two numbers:

```
<html>
<head>
</head>
</body>
<form method="post"
action="calc_procedural_code.php">
<table>
<tr><td><input type="text" name="number1"
size="10"></td></tr>
<tr><td><input type="text" name="number2"
size="10"></td></tr>
<tr><td><input type="submit" name="submit"
value="Calculate"></td></tr>
</table>
</form>
</body>
</html>
```

Save the form as a calculator.html file. Now let us write a PHP code that performs the calculation.

```
<?
//calc_procedural_code.php
 $num1=$_POST ['number1'];
 $num2=$_POST ['number2'];
 $sum=$num1 + $num2;
 $difference=$num1 - $num2;
 $multi=$num1 * $num2;
 $div=$num1/$num2;
 echo "Sum=".$sum." <br>";
 echo "Difference =".$difference." <br>";
 echo "Multiplication=".$multi." <br>";
 echo "Division=".$div."<br>";

 ?>
```

Save the file as calc_procedural_code.php. Run the calculator.html form on a web server and enter any numbers, for example, 6 and 3. Then click the calculate button, and the PHP script will display the output:

Sum = 9

Difference = 3

Multiplication = 18

Division = 2

Let us perform the same calculation by using functions in PHP code. Create file

"calc_function.php" with the following code:

```
<?
//Define functions for each calculation action
function add ($number1, $number2) {
$sum=$number1 + $number2;
return $sum;
}

function subtract ($number1, $number2) {
$dif=$number1 - $number2;
return $dif;
}

function multiply ($number1, $number2) {
$multi=$number1 * $number2;
return $multi;
}
function divide ($number1, $number2) {
$div=$number1/$number2;
return $div;
}

$num1=$_POST ['number1'];
$num2=$_POST ['number2'];
//call functions:
$sum=add ($num1, $num2);
$dif= subtract ($num1, $num2);
$multi= multiply ($num1, $num2);
$div= divide ($num1, $num2);

//Output the result
echo "Sum=".$sum." <br>";
```

```
echo "Difference =".$dif." <br>";
echo "Multiplication=".$multi." <br>";
echo "Division=".$div."<br>";
?>
```

Edit calculator.html file.
Change action="cacl_procedural_code.php"
to action="calc_function.php".
Again, run the calculator.html form on a web server and enter
----- any numbers, for example, 6 and 3. Click the calculate button, and the PHP script will display output:
Sum = 9
Difference = 3
Multiplication = 18
Division = 2

Now let us create PHP code with class.

```
<?
// define class
class Calculator {

//class variables:
var $sum;
var $dif;
var $multi;
var $div;

//Class member functions or methods:
function add ($number1, $number2) {

$this->sum=$number1 + $number2;
}

function subtract ($number1, $number2) {

$this->dif=$number1 - $number2;
}

function multiply ($number1, $number2) {
```

```
 $this->multi=$number1 * $number2;
 }

 function divide ($number1, $number2) {

 $this->div=$number1/$number2;
 }
}

 $num1=$_POST ['number1'];
 $num2=$_POST ['number2'];

 //Create a class instance:
 $calc = new Calculator ();
 //Call class methods:
 $calc->add ($num1, $num2);
 $calc->subtract ($num1, $num2);
 $calc->multiply ($num1, $num2);
 $calc->divide ($num1, $num2);

 //Display output:
 echo "Sum=". $calc->sum." <br>";
 echo "Difference =". $calc->dif." <br>";
 echo "Multiplication=". $calc->multi." <br>";
 echo "Division=". $calc->div."<br>";
 ?>
```

Save file as calc_class.php. Edit calculator.html form and type action="calc_class.php". Run the calculator.html form, enter numbers, and click the Calculate button. The calculation result will be displayed on the next page.

We are done. Download all files for this tutorial: php_class.zip.

MySQL installation and administration

Download MySQL

Select a GA version that is released.

If you happen to be running Windows in 64-bit mode, as I am, select the 64-bit Zip archive (mysql-noinstall-5.1.63-winx64.zip). Otherwise download the 32-bit zip archive 115.5M version (mysql-noinstall-5.1.63-win32.zip) for 32-bit mode operation.

MySQL is free, but you still have to register on their site to download. When filling in the form, indicate that you are student downloading for education and select the Self-Help Knowledge Base for available help.
When you submit the registration form, a page with links to the zip file is displayed.
Select the HTTP link for the closest mirror. Save zip file to your desktop.
Select the Documents tab and download a MySQL Manual.
Extract MySQL zip file to C:\mysql directory

Creating Users, Database and Tables in MySQL

```
Microsoft Window (Version 6.3.9600)
Copyright (c) 2013 Microsoft Corporation. All rights reserved.


C:\Users\Sergey>cd..

C:\Users>cd..

C:\>cd mysql

C:\mysql>cd bin

C:\mysql\bin>mysqld

_
```

Figure 12. Starting MySQL.

Open the command prompt window and go to C:\mysql\bin directory. See figure 9.
When you get there, type mysqld and press enter. MySQL is started.

Open one more command prompt window and go to C:\mysql\bin directory.

Set password to the default users

Connect to MySQL as the root user. Type mysql –u root and press enter. A welcome message is displayed with the server version and the copyright notice.

```
C:\mysql\bin>mysqld -u root
Welcome to the MySQL monitor. Commands end with ; or \g.
Your MySQL connection id is 1
Server version: 5.1.63-community MySQL Community Server (GPL)

Copyright (c) 2000, 2011, Oracle and/or its affiliates. All right
reserved.

Oracle is a registered trademark of Oracle Corporation and/or its
affiliated. Other names may be trademarks of their respective
owners.

Type 'help' or '\h' for help. Type '\c' to clear the current input
statement.

mysql> _
```

Figure 13. Accessing MySQL

MySQL has anonymous user and root user. To set passwords for these users type commands as illustrated below and hit enter:

```
mysql> SET PASSWORD FOR ' '@'localhost' =PASSWORD('pitbool');
Query OK, 0 rows affected (0.00 sec)

mysql> SET PASSWORD FOR 'root'@'localhost' =PASSWORD('Gointer3$');
Query OK, 0 rows affected (0.00 sec)

mysql>
```

Figure 14. Setting password to a user.

Select mysql database to view tables.
The user table is used for storing mysql user information.
To create a database with the name test, type:

'CREATE DATABASE TEST;'.
The database is created. To create a new user 'usr777' with password ' Arizona18', type a command as in the picture below.

```
GRANT ALL PRIVILEGES ON TEST.* TO
'user777'@'localhost' IDENTIFIED BY 'Arizona18';
```

The usr777 will access only TEST database. The root user can access any database.
To revoke privileges from a user, enter: `REVOKE ALL PRIVILEGES ON TEST.* from 'user777'@'localhost'`
To create user that has access to any database, enter command as in picture below.
GRANT ALL PRIVILEGES ON *.* means to all databases and tables.

Create Table

```
mysql>
mysql>CREATE TABLE students(
->studentid int (11) NOT NULL auto_increment,
->lastname varchar(15) NOT NULL default '',
->firstname varchar(15) NOT NULL default '',
->email varchar (30) NOT NULL default '',
->phone varchar (30) NOT NULL default '',
->age int (11) NOT NULL,
->gender varchar(6) NOT NULL default '',
->startdate date default NULL,
->PRIMARY KEY(studentid)
-> ) ENGINE=MyISAM AUTO_INCREMENT=1
DEFAULT CHARSET=latin1;

Query OK, 1 row affected (0.01 sec)

mysql>
```

Figure 15. Create a table statement.
To select database, enter 'use test'. A Database changed message is displayed. Now we can create a table. As depicted in the picture below, you can copy and paste a create table SQL statement:

The Create table statement includes the table name, and the name and data type for each column. See figure 12.

MySQL has the int data type for integers (whole numbers), VARCHAR is the data type for text strings up to 256 characters, TEXT data type is for large text, and DATE data type is for date. DATETIME data type is for date and time. TIME data type is for time. Read the list of all mysql data types in the MySQL manual.

The studentid column is the primary key of the table. The primary key is a column that must be unique. It identifies the record. Auto-increment means that each time a new record is inserted into the table, the studentid value will be increased by one. If you insert three (3) records, after which you delete them all and then insert one (1), the studentid of the record will not be one (1), but rather four (4).

The last line of the statement starting with the word ENGINE is optional.

AUTO_INCREMENT=30 means that the id of a new record inserted into the table will be started from 30.

DEFAULT CHARSET=latin1 is for English text. If you plan to use a different language, use CHARSET= utf8_general_ci. You can change it at any anytime. We will be discussing this more later.

To insert a record into the table, the insert statement is used. It has the following syntax: Insert into table (list of fields) values (list of values)

```
 Insert into students (studentid, lastname,
firstname, email, phone, age, gender, startdate)
 values
  (0, 'Will', 'John', 'jw@yahoo.com', '1282828',
21, '1990-12-31');
```

When you are inserting string or date values, you must use single quotation marks. When you are inserting numeric values, you should not use quotation marks. The Phone number column has the varchar data type, and I used single quotation marks to insert the phone number. If we defined phone number as an integer, we would not use quotation marks.

Pay attention to the date format: four-digit year—two-digit month—two-digit day, i.e., 07/11/11 becomes 2011-07-11.

In PHP, to convert date from a human format to a mysql format use the strtotime function.

```
$startdate=date ('Y-m-d', strtotime
('7/11/11'));
```

If you pass an empty string to function you will get 1969-12-31. So, you must check to determine whether it is empty or not.

```
if ($date !='')
$startdate=date ('Y-m-d', strtotime ($date));
```

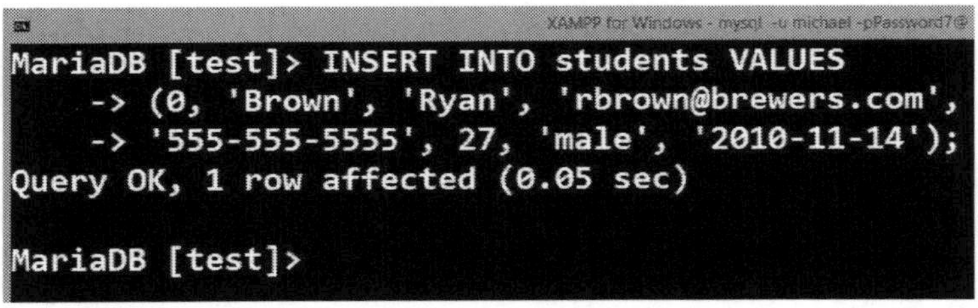

```
XAMPP for Windows - mysql -u michael -pPassword7@
MariaDB [test]> INSERT INTO students VALUES
    -> (0, 'Brown', 'Ryan', 'rbrown@brewers.com',
    -> '555-555-5555', 27, 'male', '2010-11-14');
Query OK, 1 row affected (0.05 sec)

MariaDB [test]>
```

Figure 16. Insert students

```
CREATE TABLE teachers (
 teacherid int (11) NOT NULL auto_increment,
 lastname varchar (15) NOT NULL default '',
 firstname varchar (15) NOT NULL default '',
 email varchar (30) NOT NULL default '',
 phone varchar (20) NOT NULL default '',
 hiredate date default NULL,
 rate int (11) NOT NULL default '30',
 PRIMARY KEY (teacherid)
 ) ENGINE=MyISAM AUTO_INCREMENT=6 DEFAULT
CHARSET=latin1 AUTO_INCREMENT=1;
```

Type 'exit' to exit from the mysql monitor.

Connect again as root user using the password Gointer3S. Let's create the teachers table. See figure 13.

Relationship between the tables:

There are three types of relationships between the tables in a database.

1. one to one
2. one to many
3. many to many

Let's assume, we have a students' table and a student_details table. Because the relationship between the tables is one-to-one, a single record in the student_details table will correspond with only one record in the student table. The student_details table has studentid columns that identify what specific student details record corresponds with the student record in the students table.

Let's say that we have a teachers table and a students table. One teacher may have many students, but one student has only one teacher. In that case the relationships between the tables are one-to-many. Many records in the students table will correspond with one record in the teachers table.

To handle such relationships, we'll need to add a teacherid column in the students table.

To do this, select test database, and then enter alter table statement as illustrated below.

```
Alter table students add teacherid int(11)
```

```
MariaDB [test]> ALTER TABLE STUDENTS ADD TEACHERID INT(11);
Query OK, 0 rows affected (0.52 sec)
Records: 0  Duplicates: 0  Warnings: 0
```

Figure 17. Alter table students statement.

```
MariaDB [test]>
MariaDB [test]> SHOW COLUMNS FROM STUDENTS;
+-----------+-------------+------+-----+---------+----------------
| Field     | Type        | Null | Key | Default | Extra
+-----------+-------------+------+-----+---------+----------------
| studentid | int(11)     | NO   | PRI | NULL    | auto_increment
| lastname  | varchar(15) | NO   |     |         |
| firstname | varchar(15) | NO   |     |         |
| email     | varchar(30) | NO   |     |         |
| phone     | varchar(30) | NO   |     |         |
| age       | int(11)     | NO   |     | NULL    |
| gender    | varchar(6)  | NO   |     |         |
| startdate | date        | YES  |     | NULL    |
+-----------+-------------+------+-----+---------+----------------
8 rows in set (0.18 sec)

MariaDB [test]>
```

Figure 18. The students table fields before the change.

```
MariaDB [test]> SHOW FIELDS FROM STUDENTS;
+-----------+-------------+------+-----+---------+----------------
| Field     | Type        | Null | Key | Default | Extra
+-----------+-------------+------+-----+---------+----------------
| studentid | int(11)     | NO   | PRI | NULL    | auto_increment
| lastname  | varchar(15) | NO   |     |         |
| firstname | varchar(15) | NO   |     |         |
| email     | varchar(30) | NO   |     |         |
| phone     | varchar(30) | NO   |     |         |
| age       | int(11)     | NO   |     | NULL    |
| gender    | varchar(6)  | NO   |     |         |
| startdate | date        | YES  |     | NULL    |
| TEACHERID | int(11)     | YES  |     | NULL    |
+-----------+-------------+------+-----+---------+----------------
9 rows in set (0.00 sec)
```

Figure 19. The students table fields after the change.

The statement "show fields from students" and the statement "show columns from students" are synonyms. You can use the statement "describe students" or "explain students" as well.

You will see that the teacherid column is now added to the students table.

Insert records into the teachers table.

```
Insert into teachers values (0, 'smith',
```

```
 'John', john@amail.com','727-123-1234','2000-07-
01',62);
```

It is not necessary to list column names in the insert statement. It is enough to list the values for the columns.

We inserted teacherid in the students table to implement the relationship one-to-many.

However, in reality, one student may have classes with many different teachers and one teacher may teach many students. Such relationships are called "many to many". To implement many-to-many relationships, we must create a third table with the studentid and teacherid:

```
CREATE TABLE TEACHER_STUDENT(
tstid int(11) NOT NULL AUTO_INCREMENT,
teacherid int(11) NOT NULL,
studentid int(11) NOT NULL,
PRIMARY KEY (tstid)
);
```

Now we'll remove the teacherid column from the student table:

```
 Alter table students drop column teacherid;
```

Insert teacher id and student id in the teacher_student table. First, let us view our records.

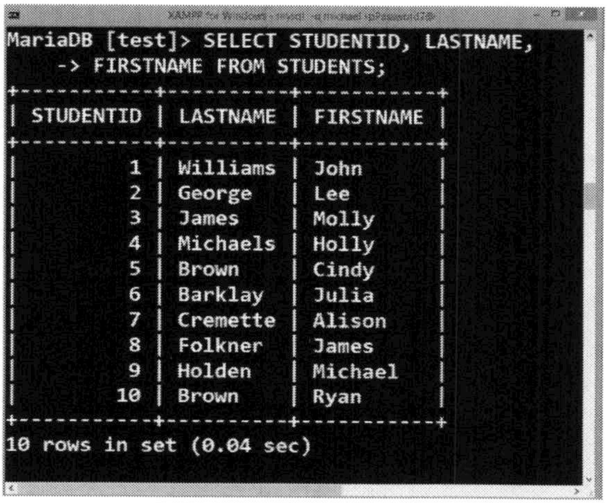

```
MariaDB [test]> SELECT STUDENTID, LASTNAME,
    -> FIRSTNAME FROM STUDENTS;
+-----------+----------+-----------+
| STUDENTID | LASTNAME | FIRSTNAME |
+-----------+----------+-----------+
|         1 | Williams | John      |
|         2 | George   | Lee       |
|         3 | James    | Molly     |
|         4 | Michaels | Holly     |
|         5 | Brown    | Cindy     |
|         6 | Barklay  | Julia     |
|         7 | Cremette | Alison    |
|         8 | Folkner  | James     |
|         9 | Holden   | Michael   |
|        10 | Brown    | Ryan      |
+-----------+----------+-----------+
10 rows in set (0.04 sec)
```

Figure 20. The students' names and ids.

From the above, we can see that Smith John id=1, and Barry James id=2. If they are students of Julia Williams, id=4, we write the following insert statements:

```
  Insert into teacher_student (tstid, teacherid, studentid)
 Values (0, 4, 1);
 Insert into teacher_student (tstid, teacherid, studentid)
 Values (0, 4, 2);
```

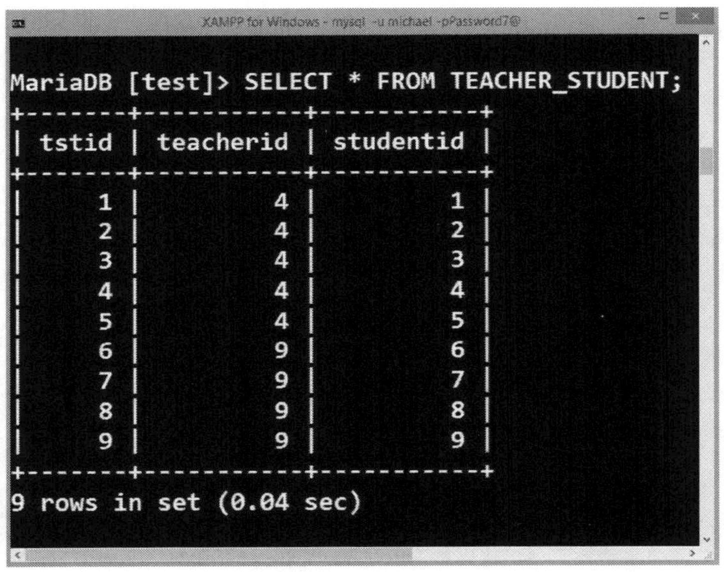

```
MariaDB [test]> SELECT * FROM TEACHER_STUDENT;
+-------+-----------+-----------+
| tstid | teacherid | studentid |
+-------+-----------+-----------+
|     1 |         4 |         1 |
|     2 |         4 |         2 |
|     3 |         4 |         3 |
|     4 |         4 |         4 |
|     5 |         4 |         5 |
|     6 |         9 |         6 |
|     7 |         9 |         7 |
|     8 |         9 |         8 |
|     9 |         9 |         9 |
+-------+-----------+-----------+
9 rows in set (0.04 sec)
```

Figure 21. The teacher_student table.

To select those students belonging to teacher Williams, we must join three tables: students, teachers and teacher_student. In a query we use studentid and teacherid to link these tables.

The query begins with SELECT word and then the list of columns we need to display.

The table name precedes the column name and the two are separated by a dot.

```
SELECT teachers.firstname, teachers.lastname,
```

```
students.firstname, students.lastname
from students, teachers, teacher_student
where
students.studentid = teacher_student.studentid
and teachers.teacherid=teacher_student.teacherid
and teachers.lastname='Williams';
```

We can make this query shorter if we substitute the table names with the letters:

```
select t.firstname, t.lastname,
s.firstname, s.lastname
from students s, teachers t, teacher_student i
where s.studentid=i.studentid
and t.teacherid=i.teacherid
and t.lastname='Williams';
```

You can concatenate fields using the CONCAT function.

```
select concat(s.firstname,' ', s.lastname) as
students, t.lastname as teacher
from students s INNER JOIN teacher_student i
ON s.studentid=i.studentid INNER JOIN teachers t
ON i.teacherid=t.teacherid and
t.lastname='Williams';
```

```
MariaDB [test]> select
    -> concat(s.firstname,' ', s.lastname) as students,
    ->  t.lastname as teacher
    -> from students s INNER JOIN teacher_student i
    -> ON s.studentid=i.studentid INNER JOIN teachers t
    -> ON i.teacherid=t.teacherid and t.lastname='Williams'
+---------------+----------+
| students      | teacher  |
+---------------+----------+
| John Williams | Williams |
| Lee George    | Williams |
| Molly James   | Williams |
| Holly Michaels | Williams |
| Cindy Brown   | Williams |
+---------------+----------+
5 rows in set (0.00 sec)
```

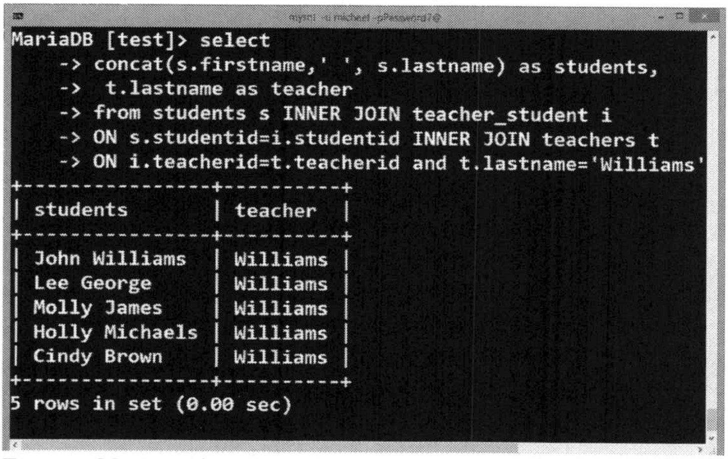

Figure 22. Display students whose teacher is Williams.

Create the courses table and insert a few records.

```
MariaDB [test]> create table course (
    -> courseid int(11) NOT NULL auto_increment,
    -> coursename varchar(50) NOT NULL default '
    -> hours int(11) NOT NULL default 100,
    -> cost float NOT NULL default 1000,
    -> PRIMARY KEY (courseid)
    -> );
Query OK, 0 rows affected (1.08 sec)

MariaDB [test]>
```

Figure 23. The course table.

```
MariaDB [test]>
MariaDB [test]>
MariaDB [test]>
MariaDB [test]> INSERT INTO COURSE
    -> (courseid,coursename,hours, cost)
    -> values
    -> (0, 'PHP', 250, 999.99 );
Query OK, 1 row affected (0.09 sec)

MariaDB [test]>
MariaDB [test]>
```

Figure 24. Insert courses.

```
MariaDB [test]> select * from course;
+----------+------------+-------+---------+
| courseid | coursename | hours | cost    |
+----------+------------+-------+---------+
|        1 | Java       |   250 |  999.99 |
|        2 | PHP        |   250 |  999.99 |
|        3 | C++        |   500 | 1999.99 |
|        4 | JavaScript |   300 | 1599.99 |
+----------+------------+-------+---------+
4 rows in set (0.00 sec)
```

Figure 25. The courses.

Again, one student can take many courses and one course may be taken by many students.

The relationships between students and courses are many-to-many. This case requires that we create a student_courses table where we place the studentid and coursid as the foreign keys.

To link students and course tables, we first create the table student_course and insert the records.

```
Database changed
MariaDB [test]> create table student_course (
    -> studentcourseid int(11) NOT NULL auto_inc
    -> studentid int(11) NOT NULL,
    -> courseid int(11) NOT NULL,
    -> paid tinyint(1) NOT NULL default 0,
    -> PRIMARY KEY (studentcourseid)
    -> );
Query OK, 0 rows affected (0.36 sec)

MariaDB [test]> _
```

Figure 26. Create the student_course table.

Insert records in the student_course table.

```
MariaDB [test]> insert into student_course
    -> (studentcourseid, studentid, courseid,
    -> paid) values(0, 2, 1, 999.99);
Query OK, 1 row affected (0.06 sec)

MariaDB [test]> insert into student_course
    -> (studentcourseid, studentid, courseid,
    -> paid) values(0, 2, 2, 999.99);
Query OK, 1 row affected (0.08 sec)

MariaDB [test]> insert into student_course
    -> (studentcourseid, studentid, courseid,
    -> paid) values(0, 3, 2, 999.99);
```

Figure 27. Insert records in the student_course table

Create the table schedule

```
MariaDB [test]> create table schedule (
    -> scheduleid int(11) NOT NULL auto_increment,
    -> courseid int(11) NOT NULL,
    -> teacherid int(11) NOT NULL,
    -> starttime time default NULL,
    -> endtime time default NULL,
    -> startdate date default NULL,
    -> PRIMARY KEY (scheduleid)
    -> );
Query OK, 0 rows affected (0.24 sec)
```

Figure 28. The schedule table.

The schedule table requires a courseid to show which course is scheduled. It must also have the teacherid to indicate which teacher will be teaching the course.

After inserting the above-mentioned values into the schedule table, we can query and view who is taking the course, at what time, who is teaching, etc.

Find a teacher name, who teaches the Java class:

```
SELECT t.firstname, t.lastname
FROM teachers t INNER JOIN schedule s ON
t.teacherid=s.teacherid INNER JOIN courses c
ON s.courseid=c.courseid
WHERE c.coursename='Java';
```

```
MariaDB [test]> SELECT t.firstname, t.lastname
    -> FROM teachers t INNER JOIN schedule s ON
    -> t.teacherid=s.teacherid INNER JOIN course c
    -> ON s.courseid=c.courseid
    -> AND c.coursename='Java';
+-----------+----------+
| firstname | lastname |
+-----------+----------+
| Julia     | Williams |
+-----------+----------+
1 row in set (0.00 sec)
```

Figure 29. A teacher who teaches Java.

Connection to MySQL with MySQLi

The old MySQL extension was deprecated as of PHP 5.5.0. For the latest PHP version, it is recommended to use PDO or MySQLi.

In my connection code example, I will use the connection to usernames table located in test database.

I have the usernames table. You can create it by using the following create table statement.

```
CREATE TABLE usernames(
      userid int (11) NOT NULL AUTO_INCREMENT,
      lastname varchar (20) DEFAULT NULL,
      firstname varchar (20) DEFAULT NULL,
      username varchar (20) DEFAULT NULL,
      password varchar (50) DEFAULT NULL,
      email varchar (30) DEFAULT NULL,
      role varchar (10) DEFAULT NULL,
      active tinyint (4) DEFAULT NULL,
      PRIMARY KEY(userid)
 );
```

After the table is created, you may use a command "show columns from usernames;" to see all its columns

Create the connect.php file with the following code. Use your host, user, password and database.

```
<?php

 $link = mysqli_connect ("localhost", "root",
"secret", "test");

 if(mysqli_connect_errno())
 {
 $msg="Failed to connect to MySQL: ".
 mysqli_connect_error ();
 }
?>
```

Later, you may include this file in any php file that accesses data in the database. To insert records in the usernames table, use the following code. insert_record.php

```
 <?php
 include ('connect.php');

 $lastname="Silver";
 $firstname="John";
 $username="johnsl";
 // md5 encrypted word "password"
 $password="5f4dcc3b5aa765d61d8327deb882cf99";
 $email="johnsl@gmail.com";
 $role="user";


 $ipsql="insert into usernames (userid, lastname,
firstname,username, password, email, role,
active)
 values
(0,'".$lastname."','".$firstname."','".$username.
"','".$password."','".$email."','".$role."' 1)";

   if (!mysqli_query ($link, $ipsql))
   {
   $msg=mysqli_error ($link);
   }
   else
   {
   $msg="record inserted successfully!";
   }
   echo $msg;
 ?>
```

Run the insert_record.php file and check in the command prompt that the record is inserted.

Select your database and type: "select * from usernames". The record is displayed. If it is not inserted, then, probably, you made a typo.

Create a display_record.php file to display the inserted record.

```
<?php
```

```
  include ('connect.php');

 $sql="select lastname, firstname,
username,email,
  role from usernames where email='".$email."'";
   if(!$uresult=mysqli_query($link, $sql))
   {
      $msg=mysqli_error ($link);
   }
   else
   {

$urow = mysqli_fetch_array($uresult, MYSQLI_NUM);

        $lastname=$urow [0];
        $firstname=$urow [1];
        $username=$urow [2];
        $email=$urow [3];
        $role=$urow [4];

echo $lastname." | " .$firstname. " | " .
$username. " | " .$role. "<br>";
}
 ?>
```

For updating the record, create the "update_record.php" file.

```
 <?php
  include ('connect.php');

 $role="admin";
 $username="sniderj";

 $sql="UPDATE usernames SET role='".$role."'
where username='".$username."'";

 //echo "sql=".$sql."<br>";

    if(!mysqli_query ($link, $sql))
    {
       $msg=mysqli_error ($link);
    }
    else
```

```
    {
       $msg="Record is updated successfully!";
    }
        echo $msg;
 ?>
```

To delete the record, create the "delete_record.php" file.

```
 <?php
 include ('connect.php');

 $userid=2;

 $sql="delete from usernames where
userid=".$userid;
 //echo "sql=".$sql."<br>";

     if (!mysqli_query($link, $sql))
     {
       $msg=mysqli_error($link);
     }
     else
     {
       $msg="Record is deleted successfully!";
     }
    echo $msg;
 ?>
```

You can create a function to insert, update or delete a record. This function will take a query as an argument that we pass by value and message argument that is passed by reference. The function returns 1 in case of success and 0 in case of failure.

```
 function execute ($sql, &$msg){

        if (!mysqli_query($link, $sql))
        {
        $msg=mysqli_error ($link);
        return 0;
        }
        else
        {
```

```
        $msg="Success!";
        return 1;
    }
}
```

You may display not only the data, but also the table column names and other metadata.

```
 <?php
 include ('connect.php');

 $email="myemail@gmail.com";

 $sql="select lastname, firstname, username,
email, role from usernames where
email='".$email."'";

if (!$result=mysqli_query ($link, $sql))
{
$msg=mysqli_error ($link);
}
else
{
  while($fieldinfo=mysqli_fetch_field($result))
  {
print ("Database: ". $fieldinfo->db. " | ");
print ("Table: ". $fieldinfo->table. " | ");
print ("Name: ". $fieldinfo->name. " | ");
print ("charset #:".$fieldinfo->charset. " | ");
print ("Length: ". $fieldinfo->length. " | ");
print ("Max_length:".$fieldinfo->max_length."|");
print ("Type: ". $fieldinfo->type. " | <br>");
  }
}
 mysqli_free_result ($result);
 ?>
```

```
 Output:
```

Database: test | Table: usernames | Name: lastname | charset #: 8 | Length: 20 | Max_Length: 6 | Type: 253 |
Database: test | Table: usernames | Name: firstname | charset #: 8 | Length: 20 | Max_Length: 4 | Type: 253 |

Database: test | Table: usernames | Name: username | charset #: 8 | Length: 20 | Max_Length: 7 | Type: 253 |
Database: test | Table: usernames | Name: email | charset #: 8 | Length: 30 | Max_Length: 17 | Type: 253 |
Database: test | Table: usernames | Name: role | charset #: 8 | Length: 10 | Max_Length: 5 | Type: 253 |

The Simplest Page View Counter

There are many PHP code examples of visitor/page view counters. To implement the simplest page counter in PHP, simply include the following script in every web page, and the number of times each page is viewed by a user will be displayed.

Create a simple table in MySQL.

```
CREATE TABLE visitors_count (
countid int (11) NOT NULL auto_increment,
count int (11) NOT NULL default '1',
page varchar (100) default NULL,
remoteip varchar (30) default NULL,
PRIMARY KEY ('countid')
) ;
```

Enter 1 as the default value for the page count field. The page field should contain a web page name. For example, PHP file name. Enter all your page names in the page field. Use query:

```
"insert into visitors_count (countid, count,
page) values (0, 1, 'index.php');
"insert into visitors_count (countid, count,
page) values (0, 1, 'nextpage');
```

If your web page is an index.html file, rename its extension to "php" and type the following at the bottom:

```
<?php
$page="index.php";
include ('counter.php');
?>
```

The above counter.php file contains the script generating the count.

```
<?php
 $count=0;
 $link=mysqli_connect ("localhost", "root",
"secret", "test");
 if(mysqli_connect_errno())
 {
  $msg="Failed to connect to MySQL: ".
  mysqli_connect_error ();
 }

$sql="select count from visitors_count where
 page='".$page."'";

if (!$result=mysqli_query($link, $sql))
{
         $msg=mysqli_error($link);
}
else
{
$row = mysqli_fetch_array($result, MYSQLI_NUM)

$count=$row[0];
echo "Visitors: ". $count."<br>";
 } //increase count by one and save

 $count=$count+1;
//update count in the table
$usql="update visitors_count set count=".
$count." where page='". $page."'";

if (!mysqli_query ($link, $ipsql))
{
   $msg=mysqli_error ($link);
}
else
{
    $msg="Record updated!";
}
?>
```

How does it work?

1. You assign a different value for the $page variable in the script you included on each of the web pages.

2. The query will pull the count value for each particular page.

3. The count number is displayed.

4. The count variable is incremented by 1 and the record is updated.

Displaying field names from Mysql Table

Here you will find a PHP code example that pulls data from a MySQL database and displays it on the form. When developing a PHP application displaying records from different tables with the different columns, numbers, and names, you must write the HTML code for each.

The PHP code example below is universal for any query.

```
<?php

$link=mysqli_connect("localhost","michael","Passw
ord7@", "test");

if (mysqli_connect_errno())
{
 $msg="Failed to connect to MySQL: " .
mysqli_connect_error();
}

$sql="select userid, lastname, firstname,
username, email, role, active from visitors order
by username";

if (!$result=mysqli_query($link, $sql))
{
          $msg=mysqli_error($link);
}
else
{
```

```
    $c=0;
        while($row = mysqli_fetch_array($result,
MYSQLI_ASSOC)) {
            if($c==0)
            {
            $headers = array_keys($row);
            print('<table><tr><th>');
          echo implode('</th><th>', $headers);
               print('</th></tr>');
               }
        print('<tr><td>');
        echo implode('</td><td>', $row);
        print('</td></tr>');
        $c++;
        }
print('</table>');
}
?>
```

Using PDO with MySQL

PDO is a Database Access Abstraction Layer, an application programming interface which unifies the communication between a computer application and different databases. In this chapter we will discuss how to use PDO with MySQL.

According to PHP.net, a PDO class has been supported in PHP since version 5.1.0

To connect to MySQL, use the following code.

pdo_conn.php

```
<?php
 $host = 'localhost';
 $db='yourdb';
 $charset = 'utf8';
 $userdb = 'youruser';
 $passdb = 'yourpassword';
 $pdo=null;
 $dsn = "mysql:host= $host;dbname= $db; charset=
 $charset";

 $options = array (
```

```
 PDO:  ATTR_ERRMODE      => PDO:
ERRMODE_EXCEPTION,
 PDO:  ATTR_EMULATE_PREPARES   => false,
 );
 try {

 $pdo = new PDO ($dsn, $userdb, $passdb,
$options);

 } catch (PDOException $e) {
 echo "Could not connect to database!";
 }
 ?>
```

Let's insert a record in our usernames table. In this code we will use the bindParam method.

pdo_insert_user.php

```
 <?php
 // insert using bindParam method
 include ('pdo_conn.php');

 $isql="insert into usernames (lastname,
firstname, username, password, email,role,
active)
 values (:lastname, :firstname, :username,
:password, :email, :role, :active)";

 $lastname="Smith";
 $firstname="John";
 $username="johnsm";
 $password="secret";
 $email="johnsm@yahoo.com";
 $role="user";

 $active=1;

 try {

$stmt = $pdo->prepare ($isql);
```

```
$stmt->bindParam(':lastname', $lastname, PDO:
PARAM_STR);
$stmt->bindParam(':firstname', $firstname, PDO:
PARAM_STR);
$stmt->bindParam(':username', $username, PDO:
PARAM_STR);
$stmt->bindParam(':password', $password, PDO:
PARAM_STR);
$stmt->bindParam(':email', $email, PDO:
PARAM_STR);
$stmt->bindParam(':role', $role, PDO:
PARAM_STR);
$stmt->bindParam(':active', $active, PDO:
PARAM_INT);

 $stmt->execute ();

 $insertId = $pdo->lastInsertId ();

 echo "LastID=".$insertId;

 echo "New records inserted successfully";
        }
         catch (PDOException $e)
        {
        echo "Error: " . $e->getMessage ();
        }
 ?>
```

Output:
LastID=1 New records created successfully
There is a second way to insert a record with PDO. In this method we are using a placeholder.
pdo_insert_user2.php

```
<?php

//insert using placeholder
 include ('pdo_conn.php');

 $isql="insert into usernames (lastname,
```

```
firstname, username,password,email,rolea,
active)
 values (?,?,?,?,?,?,?)";
 $lastname="Barry";
 $firstname="John";
 $username="johnb";
 $password="secret";
 $email="johnb@yahoo.com";
 $role="user";
 $active=1;

 try {

 $stmt = $pdo->prepare ($isql);

 //argument for execute method must be array []
 $stmt->execute ([$lastname, $firstname,
$username, $password, $email, $role, $active]);

 $insertId = $pdo->lastInsertId ();

 echo "LastID=".$insertId;

 echo "New records inserted successfully";
      }
      catch (PDOException $e)
      {
      echo "Error: " . $e->getMessage ();
      }
 ?>
```

Output:
LastID=2 New records inserted successfully
Updating a record, using the bindParameter method.
pdo_update_user.php

```
<?php
//update using bindParam method
include ('pdo_conn.php');

$isql="update usernames set role=:role where
username=:username";
```

```
$username='johnsm';
 $role="ADMIN";

try {

$stmt = $pdo->prepare ($isql);

$stmt->bindParam(':username', $username, PDO:
PARAM_STR);
$stmt->bindParam(':role', $role, PDO:PARAM_STR);

$stmt->execute ();

echo $username."'s records updated
successfully!";
      }
      catch (PDOException $e)
      {
      echo "Error: " . $e->getMessage ();
      }
?>
```

Output:
johnsm's records updated successfully!
Updating record using placeholder.
pdo_update_user2.php

```
<?php
//update using placeholder
include ('pdo_conn.php');

$usql="update usernames set role=? where
username=?";

$username='johns';

$role="OWNER";

try {

$stmt=$pdo->prepare ($usql);
```

```
 $stmt->execute ([$role, $username]);

 echo $username."'s records updated
successfully!";
       }
       catch (PDOException $e)
       {
       echo "Error: " . $e->getMessage ();
       }
 ?>
```

Output:
johnsm's records updated successfully!
Selecting users
pdo_select_user.php

```
 <?php
  include ('pdo_conn.php');

 $sql="select userid, firstname, lastname,
username, role from usernames";

         if (!$stmt=$pdo->query ($sql))
         {
         echo mysql_errno () . ": ";
         echo mysql_error () . "<br/>";
         }
         else
         {
   while ($row = $stmt->fetch (PDO:  FETCH_NUM))
             {
             $userid=$row [0];
             $firstname=$row [1];
             $lastname=$row [2];
             $username=$row [3];
             $role=$row [4];

        echo $userid."|". $firstname. "|".
$lastname." | ". $username ." | ". $role
."<br/>";

             }
```

```
        }
?>
```

Output:
11 | Barry | John | johnb | user
3 | Silver | John | johnsl | user
9 | Smith | John | johnsm | user
6 | Silver | John | johnsl | user
8 | Snider | John | johns | admin
Delete user using bindParam method.
pdo_delete_user.php

```
<?php
//delete using bindParam method
include ('pdo_conn.php');

$dsql="delete from usernames where
lastname=:lastname";

$lastname="Johnsons";

try {
$stmt = $pdo->prepare ($dsql);
$stmt->bindParam (':lastname', $lastname,
PDO:  PARAM_STR);

$stmt->execute ();

echo $lastname."'s records deleted
successfully";
     }
       catch (PDOException $e)
       {
       echo "Error: " . $e->getMessage ();
       }
?>
```

Output:
johns's records deleted successfully!
Delete user using placeholder.
pdo_delete_user2.php

```
<?php
 //delete using placeholder
 include ('pdo_conn.php');

 $dsql="delete from usernames where lastname=?";
 $lastname="Barry";

 try {

 $stmt = $pdo->prepare ($dsql);
//execute required array
 $stmt->execute ([$lastname]);
echo $lastname."'s records deleted successfully";
      }
        catch (PDOException $e)
        {
        echo "Error: " . $e->getMessage ();
        }
 ?>
```

Output:
Barry's records deleted successfully!

Displaying column's names

pdo_get_headers.php

```
 <?php
  include ('pdo_conn.php');

  $rs = $pdo->query ('SELECT * FROM usernames
LIMIT 0');

  for($i = 0; $i < $rs->columnCount(); $i++) {
        $col = $rs->getColumnMeta ($i);
        echo $col ['name']."<br/>";
        }
 ?>
```

Output: userid lastname firstname username password email role active

Generate Charts from a MySQL

August Royalties Earned Per Day

Title	Author	Price	Date	Quantity	Earning
Learn SQL By Examples	Sergey Skudaev	2.99	08/01/2019	2	5.98
Learn SQL By Examples	Sergey Skudaev	2.99	08/02/2019	2	5.98
Learn SQL By Examples	Sergey Skudaev	2.99	08/03/2019	4	11.96
Learn SQL By Examples	Sergey Skudaev	2.99	08/04/2019	2	5.98
Learn SQL By Examples	Sergey Skudaev	2.99	08/05/2019	2	5.98
Learn SQL By Examples	Sergey Skudaev	2.99	08/06/2019	1	2.99
Learn SQL By Examples	Sergey Skudaev	2.99	08/07/2019	3	8.97
Learn SQL By Examples	Sergey Skudaev	2.99	08/08/2019	3	8.97
Learn SQL By Examples	Sergey Skudaev	2.99	08/09/2019	1	2.99
Learn SQL By Examples	Sergey Skudaev	2.99	08/10/2019	4	11.96

Figure 30. Royalties Earned Per Day.

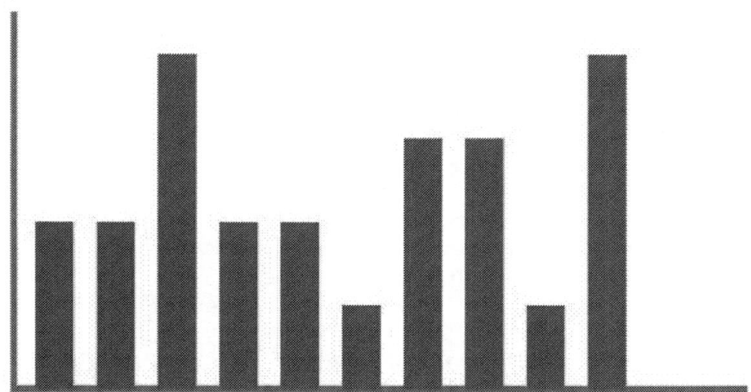

Figure 31. Royalties Earned Per Day Chart.

When I start a new project, first, I create a database and tables. In this demo project I use MySQL. The database name is mydb. The first table name is books. It contains data about a book: title, author, cost. The primary key that identifies each record is bookid. To create a table, use the following statement:

```
CREATE TABLE books (
bookid INT NOT NULL AUTO_INCREMENT,
title varchar (100),
author varchar (20),
cost DECIMAL (4,2),
PRIMARY KEY (bookid)
) ENGINE=MyISAM AUTO_INCREMENT=1 DEFAULT
CHARSET=latin1
```

The bookid data type is an integer. Auto increment means that when you insert a new record, the bookid will automatically be increased by one. (AUTO_INCREMENT=1). The title column has a string data type. The varchar (100) means that the string length is limited to 100 characters. The author column has a string data type limited to 20 characters. For currency, I use a decimal data type. It is a number with 2 decimal places. Insert data in the books table with the following SQL statements:

```
insert into books (bookid, title, author,
cost) values (1, 'Learn SQL By Examples',
'Sergey Skudaev', 2.99);
insert into books (bookid, title, author,
cost) values (2, 'PHP Programming for
Beginners', 'Sergey Skudaev', 2.99);
insert into books (bookid, title, author,
cost) values (3, 'PHP Programming for
Beginners C++ Programming By Example',
'Sergey Skudaev', 2.99);
```

The second table stores data about books sales. This table includes bookid from the first table to link the book data with the book sales data. The saleid is the primary key for the books_sales table. The sold_date is the date when the book was sold and the book_num field stores number of books sold on that date. The bookid is a foreign key from the books table. It allows one to determine which book was sold.

```
CREATE TABLE books_sales (
saleid int (11) NOT NULL AUTO_INCREMENT,
sold_date date,
book_num TINYINT,
bookid TINYINT NOT NULL,
PRIMARY KEY (saleid)
) ENGINE=MyISAM AUTO_INCREMENT=1 DEFAULT
CHARSET=latin1
```

Insert data in the books_sales table:

```
insert into books_sales (saleid, sold_date, book_num, bookid)
values (0, '2019-08-01', 2,1);
insert into books_sales (saleid, sold_date, book_num, bookid)
values (0, '2019-08-02', 2,1);
insert into books_sales (saleid, sold_date, book_num, bookid)
values (0, '2019-08-03', 4,1);
insert into books_sales (saleid, sold_date, book_num, bookid)
values (0, '2019-08-04', 2,1);
insert into books_sales (saleid, sold_date, book_num, bookid)
values (0, '2019-08-05', 2,1);
insert into books_sales (saleid, sold_date, book_num, bookid)
values (0, '2019-08-06', 1,1);
insert into books_sales (saleid, sold_date, book_num, bookid)
values (0, '2019-08-07', 3,1);
insert into books_sales (saleid, sold_date, book_num, bookid)
values (0, '2019-08-08', 3,1);
insert into books_sales (saleid, sold_date, book_num, bookid)
values (0, '2019-08-09', 1,1);
insert into books_sales (saleid, sold_date, book_num, bookid)
values (0, '2019-08-10', 4,1);
```

To pull data from books and books_sales tables we need to create a join query:

```
select books.title, books.author, books_sales.sold_date, books.cost
* books_sales.book_num as earning
```

from books **inner join** books_sales
where books.bookid= books_sales.bookid
and books.bookid=1 **order by** books_sales.sold_date;

The join query includes desired columns from the first table, the **from** keyword, the name of the first table, the **inner join** keyword, the name of the second table and **where** clause that includes criteria on how the record from the first table is related to the record of the second table and criteria which record to select. Then comes **order by** clause that tells the database how to sort records. In our case the records are sorted by sold date.
The **books.cost * books_sales.book_num as earning** means that we want to know how much we earned in one day. For that we multiply the cost of a book by the number of books sold. The "as earning" means that we want this result column titled "earning". If we did not write "as earning" then the column name would be left as "books.cost * books_sales.book_num"

We may make this query shorter by using a table alias. As an alias we can use any letter. For the books table, we use alias b and for the books_sales table we can use alias s:

```
select b.title, b.author, s.sold_date, b.cost * s.book_num as earning
from books b inner join books_sales s
where b.bookid=s.bookid and b.bookid=1
order by s.sold_date;
```

When we multiply the cost of 2.99 by the number of books sold, we will get a number with decimal places. To round the result to a whole number, we can use the CEIL SQL function (b.cost * s.book_num).

The chart.php file PHP code pulls sales data from the MySQL database and draws a bar chart.
chart.php source code:

```
<?php
$host = 'localhost';
$db='mydb';          // your database name
```

```
$charset = 'utf8';
$userdb = 'root';       //you can use root or your user
$passdb = 'Aspirin7@';  // enter you password
$titlear=array();
$authorar=array();
$m=array();
$sdatear=array();
$c=0;
$pdo=null;
$dsn = "mysql:host=$host;dbname=$db;charset=$charset";
//connection string
$options = array(
  PDO::ATTR_ERRMODE            =>
PDO::ERRMODE_EXCEPTION,
PDO::ATTR_EMULATE_PREPARES   => false,
);
try {
$pdo = new PDO($dsn, $userdb, $passdb, $options);
} catch(PDOException $e) {
     echo "Could not connect to database!";
     }
$sql="select
CEIL(b.cost * s.book_num) as earning
FROM
books b INNER JOIN books_sales s
ON b.bookid=s.bookid";
if(!$stmt=$pdo->query($sql)){
echo mysql_errno() . ": ";
echo mysql_error() . "<br/>";
}
else
{
  while($row = $stmt->fetch(PDO::FETCH_NUM)) {
  $m[$c]=$row[0];
  $c++;
  }
}
$h=270; //height of the main rectangle
$w=600; //width of the main rectangle
```

```
$bw=30; // width of the chart bar
$sp=20; // space between bars
//creating a blank image
$img=imagecreatetruecolor($w, $h+3);
//creating white image color
$white=imagecolorallocate($img, 255, 255, 255);
//creating pink image color
$pink=imagecolorallocate($img, 255, 0, 255);
//creating red image color
$red=imagecolorallocate($img, 255, 0, 0);
//drawing x - axis
imagefilledrectangle ($img, 0, 0, 5, $h+3, $pink);
//drawing y - axis
imagefilledrectangle ($img, 0, 0, $w, $h+3, $pink);
//filling main rectangle with white color
imagefilledrectangle ($img, 5, 0, $w, $h-3, $white);
for($i=0;  $i<sizeof($m);  $i++){
$n=$i+1;
$m[$i]=$m[$i]*20;  //*20 just to make bars higher and more
visible.
// drawing vertical bars with space in between
//for the first bar x1=$sp(space width), y1=$h-earning; the bar
width set by x2=$bw(bar width)
//for the second bar x1=$sp(space width) + $bw(first bar
width) + $sp(second space width)
//x2 for the second bar =$sp(space width) + $bw(first bar
width) + $sp(second space width) + $bw(second bar width)
//for the third bar x1=$sp(space width)* 3 + $bw(bar width) *
2
//for the third bar x2=$sp(space width)* 3 + $bw(bar width) *
3
// and so on...
imagefilledrectangle ($img, ($i*$bw+$sp*$n), $h-$m[$i],
($n*$bw+$sp*$n), $h, $red);
}
//setting header type
header('Content-type: image/jpeg');
//display image
imagejpeg($img);
```

```
//destroying image
imagedestroy($img);
?>
```

The display_chart.php file PHP code displays sales data in the grid (table) and displays the chart image created by the chart.php file.

display_chart.php code:

```
<!DOCTYPE html>
<html lang="en">
<head>
<meta charset="utf-8">
<style>

.page {

width:950px; margin-left:auto;margin-
right:auto;

}

.cnt {

text-align:center;

}

.tab {

border:1px solid #aaa; width:900px;

}

.tab th {

border-left:1px solid #aaa;
background-color:#ffffcc;
```

```
}

.tab td {

border-top:1px solid #aaa;
border-left:1px solid #aaa;

}

.tab td.even {

background-color:#efefef;

}

.tab td.odd {

background-color:#fefefe;

}

h2, h3 {

color: RGB (200, 0, 255);

}

</style>
</head>
<body>
<div class="page">
<h2 class="cnt">August Royalties Earned Per
Day</h2>

<?php
$host = 'localhost';
$db='mydb';// your database name
$charset = 'utf8';
```

```
$userdb = 'root'; //you can use root or your
user

$passdb = 'Aspirin7@';    // enter your
password

$titlear=array();
$authorar=array();
$m=array();
$sdatear=array();
$costar=array();
$earningar=array();
$quantityar=array();
$c=0;
$pdo=null;

$dsn =
"mysql:host=$host;dbname=$db;charset=$charse
t";

$options = array(

    PDO::ATTR_ERRMODE              =>
PDO::ERRMODE_EXCEPTION,
PDO::ATTR_EMULATE_PREPARES    => false,

);

try {

$pdo = new PDO($dsn, $userdb, $passdb,
$options);

} catch(PDOException $e) {

echo "Could not connect to database!";

}
```

```
$sql="select b.title, b.author, b.cost,
s.sold_date, s.book_num, (b.cost *
s.book_num) as earning

FROM

books b INNER JOIN books_sales s
ON b.bookid=s.bookid";

if(!$stmt=$pdo->query($sql)){

echo mysql_errno() . ": ";
echo mysql_error() . "<br/>";

}
else
{

    while($row = $stmt-
>fetch(PDO::FETCH_NUM)){

    $titlear[$c]=$row[0];
    $authorar[$c]=$row[1];
    $costar[$c]=$row[2];
    $sdatear[$c]=$row[3];
    $quantityar[$c]=$row[4];
    $earningar[$c]=$row[5];

    if($sdatear[$c] !="")

$sdatear[$c]=date('m/d/Y',
strtotime($sdatear[$c]));

    $c++;

    }
}
```

```
if($c>0)
{

print('<table class="tab">');

print('<tr><th>Title</th><th>Author</th><th>
Price</th><th>Date</th><th>Quantity</th><th>
Earning</th></tr>');

     for($i=0; $i< $c; $i++)
     {

     if($i % 2==0)

print('<tr><td
class="even">'.$titlear[$i].'</td><td
class="even">'.$authorar[$i].'</td><td
class="even">'.$costar[$i].'</td><td
class="even">'.$sdatear[$i].'</td><td
class="even">'.$quantityar[$i].'</td><td
class="even">'.$earningar[$i].'</td></tr>');

else

print('<tr><td
class="odd">'.$titlear[$i].'</td><td
class="odd">'.$authorar[$i].'</td><td
class="odd">'.$costar[$i].'</td><td
class="odd">'.$sdatear[$i].'</td><td
class="odd">'.$quantityar[$i].'</td><td
class="odd">'.$earningar[$i].'</td></tr>');

     }

print('</table>');

print('<h3>August Royalties Earned Per Day
Chart</h3>');
```

```
print('<img src="chart.php">');
}

?>

<br><br>
</div>
</body>
</html>
```

PHP Form with Array of Fields

In this tutorial, you will learn how to create an array of input type fields on a PHP form when you don't have advance knowledge of how many records are in the table. Records from a table or query will be displayed on the editable form. A user may edit all field data at once and save changes in the database.
Create a table in MySQL

```
create table credit_cards (
 cardid INT NOT NULL AUTO_INCREMENT,
 name varchar (20),
 type varchar (20),
 expired date,
 card_num INT,
 credit float,
 phone varchar (12),
 address varchar (100),
 city varchar (20),
 state varchar (2),
 zip varchar (10),
 PRIMARY KEY (cardid)
 );
```

Connect to MySQL and insert a few records in the table using SQL query.
"insert into credit_cards (cardid, name, type, expired,

card_num, credit, phone, address, city, state, zip) values (0,

'CHASE', 'Visa', '2008-01-01',123456789, 10000, '123-345-6789', '12 West 19 Street', 'New York','NY','10021')";

"insert into credit_cards (cardid, name, type, expired, card_num, credit, phone, address, city, state, zip) values

(0,'CITI', 'Mastercard', '2010-01-01', 192837465, 5000, '123-345-1234', '18 West 69 Street', 'New York','NY','10028')";

"insert into credit_cards (cardid, name, type, expired, card_num, credit, phone, address, city, state, zip) values(0, 'American Express', 'Mastercard', '2010-01-01',987654321, 8000, '123-345-4321', '8 West 9 Street', 'New York','NY','10028')";

A PHP form with array of input type fields is almost the same as a regular PHP form. The difference is that an input type name must have square brackets. For example:

```
<input type="text" name="myfield[]"/ >
```

The number of records has to be counted and the count must pass to the next page in the hidden input type as in the following:

```
print('<input type="hidden" name="rec_count"
value="'. $rec_count .'">);
```

In a template that inserts or updates records, you need to execute a query in loop as follows:

```
for ($i=0; $i<$rec_count; $i++)
{
```

```
 $sql="update mytable set myfield='".
$myfield[$i]."'";

        if(!mysqli_query ($link, $ipsql))
        {
         $msg=mysqli_error ($link);
        }
        else
        {
        $msg="record inserted successfully!";
        }
}
```

Download fieldarray.zip from
http://learn-coding.today/phpbook/fieldarray.zip
archive with php files.
Edit mysql access variables on both php files. Type your hostname (if not localhost), type your username (using the root user is not recommended), type in your password and database name.
$hostname="localhost";
$dbuser="root";
$dbpassword="aspirin";
$dbname="credit";

Copy these files in the fieldsarray folder in the htdocs directory on your PC. Start the example by typing the following url into the browser:

```
"http://localhost/fieldsarray/fieldsarray.php"
```

Form with the data from the credit_cards table displays. Edit field values and press the Update button. All records will be updated and displayed on the form. Experiment with the code.

Sending Mail PHP code example

You may wish to offer a means by which website visitors can send questions or suggestions about your website or your service. This can be done by creating a form.

```
 <h1>Contact Us</h1>
 <form method="post" name="myform"
action="act_about.php" >
 <ul>
 <li>
 Your Name:<input type="text" name="name"
size="30"/>
 </li>
 <li>
 Your Email:<input type="text" name="email"
size="30"/>
 </li>
 <li>
 Subject<input type="text" name="subject"
size="30"/>
 </li>
 <li>
 <textarea name="message" rows="10"
cols="60"></textarea>
 </li>
 <li>
 <input type="submit" name="submit" value="Send"
/>
 </li>
 <li><input type="reset" name="reset"
value="Reset"/>
 </li>
 </form>
```

A visitor fills in the form and presses the submit button.
The act_about.php file performs the task of sending out an email.

```
 <?php
 //declare variables
 $vname=""; //visitor name
 $message=""; //visitor message
 $vemail=""; //visitor email
 $domain_email="admin@yoursite.com";

// read variable values from POST method
 if (isset ($_POST ['name']))
 $vname=$_POST ['name'];
```

```
 if (isset ($_POST ['subject']))
 $subject=$_POST ['subject'];

 if (isset ($_POST ['email']))
 $vemail=$_POST ['email'];

 if (isset ($_POST ['message']))
 $message=$_POST ['message'];

 //append visitor email to the message
 $message=$message.'<br />'. $vemail;

 // To send HTML mail, the Content-type header
must be set
 $headers = 'MIME-Version: 1.0' . "\r\n";
 $headers .= 'Content-type: text/html;
charset=utf-8'. "\r\n";
 $headers .='From: '. $domain_email . "\r\n";
 $parameter='-f'. $domain_email;

 //wrap message to break text line after 70 chars
 $message = wordwrap($message,70, "<br />\n");

 //mail returns true if message sent successfully
 $sent = mail ($domain_email, $subject, $message,
$headers, $parameter);

 If ($sent)
 echo="You message is sent. Thank you.";

 include ('about.php');
```

Send my page to a friend

```
$sitelink="http://www.learn-coding.today/".
$page;

print ('<form method="post"
action="act_send_page_link.php">');
print ('<table align="center">');
print ('<tr><th>Send message to your friend about
this page. </th></tr>');
```

```
print ('<tr><td>Your Email: <input type="text"
 name="youremail"/></td></tr>');
 print ('<tr><td>Friend Email: <input type="text"
name="email" />
 print ('<input type="hidden" name="page"
value="'. $page.'"/></td></tr>');
 print ('<tr><td>Subject:<input type="text"
name="subject"/></td></tr>');
 print ('<tr><td><textarea name="message"
rows="3" cols="40"></textarea></td></tr>');
 print ('<tr><td>');
 print ('<input type="hidden" name="sitelink"
value="`. $sitelink.'"/> 76
 print ('<input type="hidden" name="linktitle"
value="'.$linktitle.'"/>
 print ('<input type="hidden" name="pageid"
value="'. $pageid. '"/></td></tr>');
 print ('<td><input type="submit" name="submit"
value="Send"/></td></tr>');
 print ('</table></form>');
```

act_send_page_link.php:

```
 <?php
 $email=$_POST ['email'];
 $youremail=$_POST ['youremail'];
 $message=$_POST ['message'];
 $youremail=htmlspecialchars($youremail,
 ENT_QUOTES);
 $email=htmlspecialchars($email, ENT_QUOTES);
 $message=htmlspecialchars($message, ENT_QUOTES);
 $item=$_POST ['linktitle'];
 $sitelink=$_POST ['sitelink'];
 $page=$_POST ['page'];
 $message .='<br>';
 $message .='<a
 href="'.$sitelink.'">'.$sitelink.'</a><br>';
 $message .='<br>';
 $subject=$_POST ['subject'];
 $subject=htmlspecialchars ($subject,
ENT_QUOTES);
 $pageid=$_POST ['pageid'];
```

```
 if (! isset ($pageid))
 $pageid=1; //assume that home page has pageid=1;
 $parameter = '-f'. $youremail;

 if ($subject=="")
 $subject="Cool tutorial!";

 if(($email=="")||($youremail==""))
 {
 print ('Please go back and enter email
addresses. <a href="'. $sitelink .'">Go
back</a>');
 }
else
 {
 $headers = 'MIME-Version: 1.0' . "\r\n";
 $headers .= 'Content-type: text/html;
charset=ISO-8859-1' . "\r\n";
 $headers .='From: ';
 $headers .=$youremail. "\r\n";

 mail ($email, $subject, $message, $headers,
$parameter);
 ?>
```

User Registration and Authentication (PDO)

I am offering a set of PHP templates for your website authentication for free. Templates are included in the responsive_website.zip file. Additionally, a style.css file is included for a three-columned page layout and web page template.

User Registration and Authentication includes the following steps:

1. User enters his or her username, first name, last, name and email address.
2. User clicks Submit button. The System validates data entered by the user. I use JavaScript for validation.

3. The system checks if the username is unique.

4. If data is valid and username is unique, the record is saved to the database and the confirmation link is sent to the user's email.

5. If data is not valid or the username is already taken, a message is displayed, and the record is not saved to the database. The user has to enter a new username, fix invalid data and submit the form again.

6. If the data is valid and a new username is unique, the record is saved to the database and the confirmation link is sent to the user's email.

7. The user opens the email, clicks the confirmation link and the user account is activated. Now the user can log in on the sign_in page.

8. If the user forgot the password, the user can click the Forgot password link and a form with username and email fields is displayed. The user enters the username and the email and clicks the Send Password button. A new password will be sent to the user's email.

9.The user may log in on the sign_in page and then change the password.

The responsive_website.zip file includes the complete PHP code that supports all steps listed above.

Download it from here:

http://learn-coding.today/phpbook/responsive_website.zip. To make your website capable of registering visitors and setting different permissions to visitors, you have to perform the following steps.

1. Create a mail account on your hosting control panel.

How to set an email account in your control panel visit this web page:

http://learn-coding.today/hosting_control_panel.php

2. Create a MySQL database and database users.

Read here
http://www.learn-coding.today/cpanel_mysql_setup.php

3. Create a usernames table in the MySQL database using phpMyAdmin. Detailed instructions will be provided.

Your hosting control panel has phpMyAdmin installed. You can use it right away to access your database and create tables. Open the SQL window and paste the script I've included in the visitors.sql.txt file. Click the Go button and the visitors table will be created.

4. Edit the "connect.php" file. Enter your database name, your username, and your user password created in step 2. Enter your hosting email address created in step 1.

It should look like the following:

```
<?php
 // PHP Data Objects(PDO)
 require_once ('includes/errors.php');
 $host = 'localhost';
 $db='test'; // your database name
 $charset = 'utf8';
 $userdb = 'michael';//you can use root or user
 $passdb = 'Password7@'; // enter your password

 $pdo=null;
 $dsn =
"mysql:host=$host;dbname=$db;charset=$charset";

 $options = array (
     PDO: ATTR_ERRMODE => PDO: ERRMODE_EXCEPTION,
     PDO: ATTR_EMULATE_PREPARES => false,
 );

 try {

 $pdo =new PDO($dsn, $userdb, $passdb, $options);

 } catch (PDOException $e) {
 echo "Could not connect to database!";
 }
 $site_email="tutor@hardstuffez.com";

 ?>
```

There should be no space characters after ?> tag or before <?php tag.

If you want your particular web page to be only accessible to registered users, include the "auth.php" file on the top of this page.

The web page must have extension.php, not .html.

If you want your particular web page to be only accessible to admin users, include the "adminauth.php" file on the top of this page.

auth.php

```
<?php
 if(!isset($_COOKIE ['user'])) {
 header ("Location: sign_in.php");}

 ?>
```

If the user is not set in cookie, the sign in page is displayed.

adminauth.php:

```
 <?php
 if((!isset($_COOKIE ['role']))||($_COOKIE
['role'] != 'admin'))
 header ("Location: sign_in.php");
 ?>
```

If the role is not set in cookie or role doesn't equal 'admin', the sign_in page is displayed.

The sign_in.php file includes the metaheader.php file with HTML meta data and links to CSS and JavaScript files. I will not discuss CSS and JavaScript here. I plan to write my next book about front-end and back-end web development, where I will explain CSS and JavaScript.

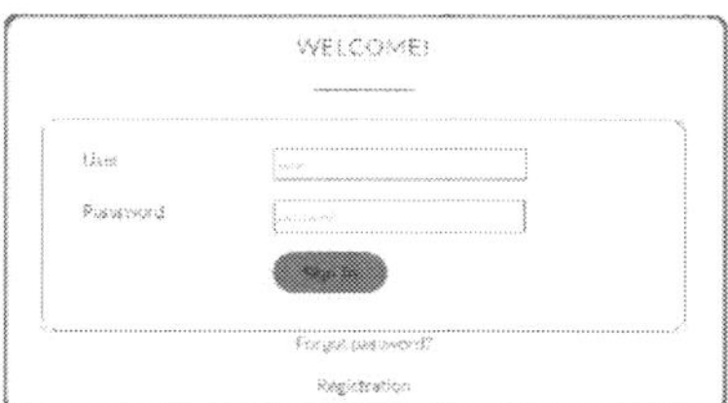

Figure 32. Login form.

This is the sign_in.php file:

```
<?php
$title="sign in";
include ('includes/metaheader.php');
$msg="";
if (isset ($_GET ['msg']))
$msg=$_GET['msg'];
?>
<script>
//validate user input
//function makes border color red if user data
is invalid and displays message.
function valForm ()
{
   var val_error=0;
var username = document.getElementById
('username');
var password=document.getElementById
('password');

 if (username.value.length==0)
 {
      username.style.border="3px solid red";
      val_error++;
 }
 else if (username.value.length >20)
 {
      username.value="20 chars allowed!";
      username.style.color="#ff9999";
      val_error++;
  }
  else if(username.value=="20 chars allowed!")
  {
      username.style.border="3px solid red";
              val_error++;
              }

      if(password.value.length==0)
```

```
        {
          password.style.border="3px solid red";
               val_error++;
               }
            if (val_error > 0)
           return false;
           else
           return true;
 }
```

//The function returns color to default and removes the message,
//when user places the cursor inside the field.

```
 function toDefault (x)
 {
 x.style.color="black";
 x.style.border="1px solid #aaa";
 if(x.value=="20 chars allowed!")
 x.value="";
 }

 </script>
 <?php

 print ('</head>');
 print ('<body>');
 print ('<div class="page-wrap">');
 print ('<div class="head-cover">');
 print ('<div class="row">');
     print ('<div class="column one-fifth">');
     print ('</div>'); // 1/5
     print ('<div class="column four-fifths">');
 include ('includes/top_nav.php');
     print ('</div>');
 print ('</div>'); // row
 print ('</div>'); // cover
 print ('<section class="start-fixed js--start-
fixed">');
 print ('<div class="page_body">');
 include ('includes/message.php');
 print ('<div class="row">');
 print ('<h2>Welcome!</h2>');
 print ('</div>');
```

```
 ?>
 <form method="POST" action="login.php"
class="contact-form">
 <div class="row">
         <div class="column w-1-3">
         <label for="username">User</label>
         </div>
         <div class="column w-2-3">
         <input type="text" name="username"
id="username" placeholder="User"
required onfocus="toDefault (this);">
     </div>
     </div>
     <div class="row">
         <div class="column w-1-3">
         <label for="password">Passsword</label>
         </div>
         <div class="column w-2-3">
         <input type="password" name="password"
id="password" placeholder="password" required
onfocus="toDefault (this);">
         </div>
     </div>
     <div class="row">
         <div class="column w-1-3">
         <label> </label>
         </div>
         <div class="column w-2-3">
         <input type="submit" name="submit"
value="Sign In" onclick="return valForm ();">
         </div>
     </div>
 </form>
 <div class="row">
     <p class="cnt">
<a href="forgot_password.php">Forgot
password?</a> </p>
     <p class="cnt"> </p>
     <p class="cnt"><a
href="enter_member.php">Registration</a></p>
 </div>
 <div class="row"> </div>
 <div class="row"> </div>
```

```
<div class="row"> </div>
<div class="row"> </div>
</div>
</div><!--page_body-->
</section>
</div><!--page_wrap-->
<?php
print ('<div class="site-footer">');
include('includes/bottommenu.php');
?>
</div>
</body>
</html>
```

Sign_in.php is just a simple form with a two text fields username and password.

To register, a visitor will need to select a Registration link to display the enter_member.php file containing a form for entering the user data.

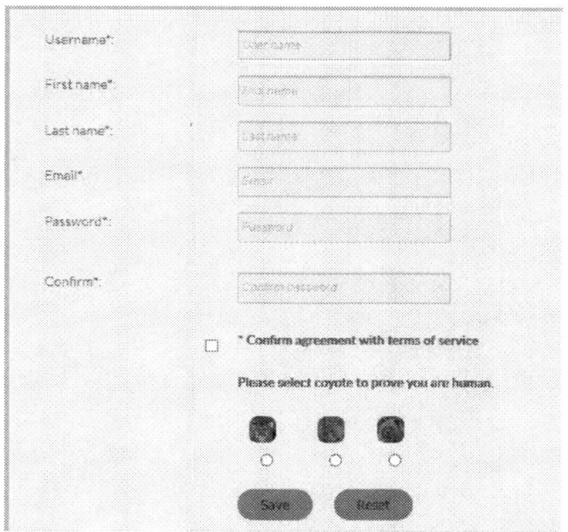

Figure 33. The registration web page

The enter_member.php file:

```
<?php
 include ("includes/conn.php");
 include ('includes/metaheader.php');
 $username="";
```

```
$firstname="";
$lastname="";
$email="";
$city="";
$country="";
$bio="";
?>
</head>
<body>
<?php
 if ($username=="")
$username=$newusername;

print ('<div class="page-wrap">');
print ('<div class="head-cover">'); // row cover
print ('<div class="row">'); //row 1
include ('includes/top_nav.php');
print ('</div>'); // row 1
print ('</div>');

$msg="";
$in=0;

if (isset ($_GET ['in']))
$in=$_GET['in'];

if ($in==1)
{
if(isset($_GET['username']))
$username=$_GET['username'];

if(isset($_GET['firstname']))
$firstname=$_GET['firstname'];

if(isset($_GET['lastname']))
$lastname=$_GET['lastname'];

if(isset($_GET['email']))
$email=$_GET['email'];
}

if(isset($_GET['msg']))
$msg=$_GET['msg'];
```

```
 include ('includes/message.php');

print ('<div class="row">'); // row 2
print ('<h3 class="cnt">Sign Up</h3>');
print ('</div>'); // row 2
print ('<section class="start-fixed">');
print ('<form method="POST" name="myform"
id="frmMain" action="act_insert_member.php">');
print ('<div class="row aform">'); //row 3
print ('<div class="row"> </div>');
print ('<div class="row">'); //row 4
print ('<div class="column w-2-5">');
print ('<label class="reg"
for="username">Username*: </label>');
print ('</div>');
print ('<div class="column w-3-5">');
print ('<input type="text" name="username"
id="username" value="'.$username.'"
onfocus="toDefault (this);" class="txt"
placeholder="Username" required>');
     print ('</div>');
print ('</div>'); // row 4

print ('<div class="row">'); //row 5
print ('<div class="column w-2-5">');
print ('<label class="reg" for="firstname">First
name*:</label>');
print ('</div>');

print ('<div class="column w-3-5">');
print ('<input type="text" name="firstname"
id="firstname" onfocus="toDefault (this);"
class="txt" placeholder="First name"
value="'.$firstname.'" required >');
print ('</div>');
print ('</div>'); // row 5
print ('<div class="row">'); // row 6
print ('<label class="reg" for="lastname">Last
name*:</label>');
print ('</div>');
print ('<div class="column w-3-5">');
```

```
print ('<input type="text" name="lastname"
id="lastname" onfocus="toDefault (this);"
class="txt" placeholder="Last name"
value="'.$lastname.'" required >');
print ('</div>');
print ('</div>'); //row 6

print ('<div class="row">'); // row 7
print ('<div class="column w-2-5">');
print ('<label class="reg" for="email">Email*:
</label>');
print ('</div>');
print ('<div class="column w-3-5">');
print ('<input type="email" name="email"
id="email" onfocus="toDefault (this);"
class="txt" placeholder="Email"
value="'.$email.'" required >');
print ('</div>');
print ('</div>'); // row 7
?>

<div class="row"> <!-- row 8 -->
<div class="column w-2-5">
<label class="reg" for="password1">Password*:
</label>
</div>
<div class="column w-3-5">
<div><input type="password" name="password1"
id="password1" onfocus="toDefault(this,
'strength_box1');" class="txt"
placeholder="Password" value="<?php echo
$password1; ?>" required ></div>
<div id="strength_box1"><div id="strength1">
</div><div id="quality"></div></div>
</div>
</div> <!-- row 8 -->

<div class="row"> <!-- row 9 -->
<div class="column w-2-5">
<label class="reg" for="password2">Confirm*:
</label>
 </div>
 <div class="column w-3-5"> <!-- row 3/4 -->
```

```
 <div><input type="password" name="password2"
id="password2" onfocus="toDefault (this,
'strength_box2');" class="txt"
placeholder="Confirm password" value="<?php echo
$password2; ?>" required ></div>
<div id="strength_box2"><div
id="strength2"></div><div id="quality2"></div>
</div></div> <!-- row 3/4 -->
 </div> <!-- row 9 -->

 <div class="row"> <!-- row 10 -->
 <div class="column w-2-5">
 <input type="checkbox" name="agree" id="agree"
onfocus="toDefault (this);" style="float:right;"
required >
</div>
<div class="column w-3-5">
<h5>* Confirm agreement with terms of
service</h5>
</div>
</div> <!-- row 10--->

 <div class="row"> <!--row 11-->
 <div class="column w-2-5"></div>
 <div class="column w-3-5">
 <h5 id="msg"></h5>
 <h4 id="invalid_choice"></h4>
 </div>
 </div> <!--row 11-->
 <div class="row"> <!--row 12-->
 <div class="column w-2-5"></div>
 <div class="column w-3-5"> <!--1/2-->
 <div class="row"> <!--row inside half-->
 <div class="column one-quarter"></div>
 <div class="column half" onclick="toDefault
(this);" id="beast">
<div class="column one-third tooltip">
<span class="tooltiptext">Lion</span>
<img src="resources/img/lionccdark.jpg"
style="height:45px;" class="captcha-img" alt=""/>
<input type="radio" name="choice" id="lion"
value="lion" class="animal"/></div>
<div class="column one-third tooltip">
```

```
<img src="resources/img/coyoteccdark.jpg"
style="height:45px" alt="" class="captcha-img"/>
<span class="tooltiptext">Coyote</span>
<input type="radio" name="choice" id="coyote"
value="coyote" class="animal"/></div>
<div class="column one-third tooltip">
<img src="resources/img/bearccdark.jpg"
style="height:45px" alt="" class="captcha-img"/>
<span class="tooltiptext">Bear</span>
<input type="radio" name="choice" value="bear"
id="bear" class="animal"/></div></div>
<div class="column one-quarter"></div>
</div> <!--row inside 3/5-->
</div> <!--3/5-->
<input type="hidden" name="animal" id="animal"
/><input type="hidden" name="selected"
id="selected" /></div> <!--row 12-->

<div class="row"> <!--row 13-->
<div class="column w-2-5"></div><!--2/5 row 13-->
<div class="column w-3-5"> <!--3/5 row 13-->
<input type="submit" id="submitbtn" name="submit"
value="Save" onclick="return valForm ();">
<input type="reset" name="clear" value="Reset"
onclick="resetAll();" >
</div> <!--3/5 row 13-->
</div> <!--row 13-->
</div> <!--3-->
</form>
</section>
</div>
</div>
<br><br><br><br><br><br><br>
<?php
print ('<div class="site-footer">');
include ('includes/bottommenu.php');
?>
</div>
```

```
<script>
$('input [type="radio"]').on('change',
function(){
      if ($(this).is(':checked'))
      $ ('#selected').val($(this).val());
 });

 </script>
 </body>
 </html>
```

If the visitor enters the correct data in the form and submits the form, the act_insert_member.php file is displayed because the form action="act_insert_member.php". This file reads from the POST method the data entered by the user on the form.

The **act_insert_member.php** file includes the **insert_visitor_indb.php** file that inserts the record into the visitors' table.
The insert_visitor_indb.php:

```
<?php
 //include ("includes/pdo_conn.php");
  $role="user";
 $userid_count=0; //Check if username is taken by
exiting user.
 $sql="select count(userid) from visitors where
username='".$username."'";
 $userid_count=$pdo->query($sql)->fetchColumn();

//if username does not exist insert the user
//record
    if ($userid_count==0)
    {
 $ipsql="insert into visitors (userid, firstname,
lastname, username, password, email, role,
active)
 values
  (0,'".$firstname."', '".$lastname."',
'".$username."', '".$password."', '".$email."',
'".$role."',0)";
        try {
        $userid=0;
        $active=0;
```

```
        $stmti = $pdo->prepare ($ipsql);

$stmti->bindParam (':userid', $userid, PDO:
PARAM_STR);
$stmti->bindParam (':firstname', $firstname, PDO:
PARAM_STR);
$stmti->bindParam (':lastname', $lastname, PDO:
PARAM_STR);
$stmti->bindParam (':password', $password, PDO:
PARAM_STR);
$stmti->bindParam (':email', $email, PDO:
PARAM_STR);
$stmti->bindParam (':role', $role, PDO:
PARAM_STR);
$stmti->bindParam (':active', $active, PDO:
PARAM_STR);
$stmti->execute ();

 //after record inserted, email
 //with confirmation link is sent to the user.

include ('sendmail.php');
}
        catch (PDOException $e)
       {
$msg="Something went wrong. Your record was not
saved!";
$msg=$msg." Error: ". $e->getMessage();

 header ("Location: enter_member.php?in=1
&username=". $username . "&lastname=". $lastname
."&firstname=". $firstname ."&email=". $email .
"&msg=". $msg);
       }
}
else
{
$msg="The username is taken! Please enter a
different username!";
```

```
 header ("Location: enter_member.php?in=1
&username=". $username . "&lastname=". $lastname
."&firstname=". $firstname ."&email=". $email
."&msg=". $msg);
    }
 ?>
```

The visitor data is entered in the database and the sendmail.php page is called. This page sends an activation email to the visitor. The visitor opens the email, clicks the activation link, and activates her account. The visitors table has an active field equals to 0 prior to the user activation, but the field's value is updated to 1 upon the activation. If the username is taken, the form for entering user data is displayed again with all fields filled with the previously entered data. The user should enter a different username.

The sendmail.php code:

```
<?php

 $url = $_SERVER ['HTTP_HOST']. dirname ($_SERVER
['PHP_SELF']);

 include ("connect.php");

 $subject = 'User Activation';
 // To send HTML mail, the Content-type header
must be set
 $headers = 'MIME-Version: 1.0'. "\r\n";
 $headers .= 'Content-type: text/html;
charset=windows-1251' . "\r\n";
$headers. ='From: '. $domain_email . "\r\n";
 $parameter='-f'. $domain_email;
 $message ='Click this link to activate your
account<br>'.
 $url.'/activate.php?username='. $newusername;
 $message = wordwrap ($message, 70);

 mail ($email, $subject, $message, $headers,
$parameter);
```

```
if ($sent)
$msg="Please check your <b>".$email." </b>
email.";
else
$msg="Error, the confirmation email was not
sent!";
header ("Location:sign_in.php?msg=".$msg);
?>
```

An email containing a link to the activate.php script is sent to the visitor's email.

When activated, 1 is inserted into the active field.

activate.php

```
<?
include ("includes/conn.php");

$username="";

if(isset($_GET['username']))
$username=$_GET['username'];

$esql="Update visitors SET active=1 where
username=:username";

try {

$stmt=$pdo->prepare ($esql);

$stmt->bindParam (':username', $username, PDO:
PARAM_STR);

$msg=$username."´s records updated successfully!";
    }
        catch (PDOException $e)
        {
        $msg="Error: " . $e->getMessage ();
        }

$msg=$username.", Your account is activated.";
```

```
header ("Location: sign_in.php?msg=".$msg);
}
?>
```

After execution of the activate.php file, the sign_in.php page is displayed. After that the "Your account is activated." message is displayed. Or an error message is displayed if the update failed.

When a user account is activated, the user can log in on the sign in page. The username and password are submitted to the login.php script. The login.php script checks if the username record with the username and password exists in the visitors table. If the record exists, the value of the active field is then checked to ascertain whether the user is active.

An email containing the activation link is sent to the user if active=0. However, if active=1, the user profile page is displayed. If the record doesn't exist, the sign in page is displayed with the message that username or password is incorrect.

login.php

```
<?php

 include ("includes/conn.php");
 $active=0;
 $email="";
 $sql="";
 $userdb="";
 $username = $_POST ['username'];
 $password = $_POST ['password'];

 setcookie ("user","");
 setcookie ("role","");

 //md5 ('password')=
//'f4dcc3b5aa765d61d8327deb882cf99'

 $password=md5($password);

 $auth = false; // Assume user is not
authenticated

 if((isset($username))&&(isset($password)))
```

```
 {
   $sql = "SELECT username, password, role FROM
visitors WHERE username = '". $username ."' AND
password = '". $password. "' AND active=1";

 if (!$stmt=$pdo->query($sql))
 {
    echo mysql_errno (). ": ";
    echo mysql_error (). "<br/>";
 }
 else
 {
     if($row = $stmt->fetch (PDO:  FETCH_NUM))
     {
       $auth=true;
       $userdb=$row [0];
       $passodb=$row [1];
       $roledb=$row [2];

       setcookie ("user","");
       setcookie ("role","");
       setcookie ("user", $userdb);
       setcookie ("role", $roledb);

  //if user exists and active display profile
       $msg.=" Welcome to our site!";
header("Location:act_myprofile.php?msg=".$msg.
"&page=login.php");
     }
     else
     $msg.=" No result! ";
 }

 if(!$auth)
 {
  $asql ="SELECT active, email FROM visitors
WHERE username = '". $username."' AND password =
'". $password. "'";

       if (!$stmt=$pdo->query ($asql))
       {
            echo mysql_errno (). ": ";
            echo mysql_error (). "<br/>";
```

```
            }
            else
            {
            $row = $stmt->fetch (PDO:  FETCH_NUM);
            $active=$row [0];
            $email=$row [1];
            }
           //if user exists and not active
if (($active !=1)&& ($email !=""))
{
   $crnl="\r\n";
   $subject = 'User Activation';
   $headers = 'MIME-Version: 1.0'. $crnl;
$headers .= 'Content-type: text/html; char
set=iso-8859-1'. $crnl;
$headers .='From: '. $site_email. $crnl;
$parameter='-f'. $site_email;

       $msg.="Click this link to activate your
account<br/>
http://www.myearth.com/activate.php?username=".
$username;

$msg= wordwrap ($message, 70);

   mail ($email, $subject, $message, $headers,
$parameter);
$msg.=" Your account is not active. Please check
your email and activate your account.". $sql;

header("Location:sign_in.php?msg=". $msg);
}
else
{
 $msg.=" Your login or password is not correct!";

header("Location:sign_in.php?msg=". $msg);
}
} // if not auth

} else {
     $msg.="Please enter login and password!";
     header ("Location:sign_in.php?msg=". $msg);
```

```
}
?>
```

To make a page or file accessible only to those users having an admin role, set your role to admin when you register yourself. This can be done in phpMyAdmin. Open the username table, find your record and change your role from user to admin. All other users will have their role set to that of a regular user, which will allow them no access to admin pages. See the above on how to use phpMyAdmn.

I include style.css files to control web page design and layout and JavaScript files for user input validation.

Test your website user registration by creating your account, login and password. Once the email with the activation link is sent to your user email, open the email and click the activation link to activate your account. Then login to your website.

Please be aware that the use of login and password, by your website users, affecting access to certain web pages, does not mean your pages are secure. And further, the difference between a secured versus an insecure connection will depend on what type of Hypertext Transfer Protocol is being used. The use of a https transfer protocol means that the data being transferred between the web server and client browser is encrypted. But if a http type of protocol is being used; the data transfer is not being encrypted.

In the past, an insecure HTTP protocol was sufficient for use with login and password for personal, social sites, etc. Today, Goggle encourages web masters to use HTTPS.

Banking sites require absolute security and so will use an HTTPS transfer protocol. However, if your site is not a banking one, an HTTP protocol is fine for use with login and password.

It is fine even for business sites. Display your products or services on insecure pages, but when your user needs to enter a payment have them redirected to a secured page. My website uses an insecure HTTP protocol; however, a PayPal secured page is used to accept payments.

Download responsive_website.zip file (http://www.learn-coding.today/phpbook/responsive_website.zip) with all the required source code files including PHP, JavaScript and CSS.

PHP: Functional Programming

Since PHP version 5.3, PHP supports functional programming. What does it mean? We could create functions in PHP before. What is the difference? The difference is that now we can assign a function to a variable or pass it as a parameter to a new function. Let's look at the following example of PHP code that converts Fahrenheit temperature to Celsius.

```
<?php
// function-variable that return value
function getFr () {

return 95;

}

// create anonymous (Lambda) function converting F to C

function ($f) {

//converting Fahrenheit to Celsius and
//rounding result to a whole number

return (round ( ($f-32)* (5/9),0));
};
```

Since the anonymous function does not have a name, to call it we have to assign it to a variable. A function that can be assigned to a variable is called the Lambda function.

```
$C = function ($f) {

return(round(($f-32)* (5/9),0));

};

//Call function assigned to $C
echo '$C (getFr ());='. $C (getFr ());
?>
```

Output: $C (getFr ()); =35
We can modify the variable function in the following way:

```
function getF ($t) {

return $t;

}

// we can assign the function to a variable:
$F = getF (90);

echo $F."<br>"; // output: 32

//Again, creating a lambda function:

$C = function ($f){

return (round ( ($f-32)* (5/9),0));

};

//Call $C and pass $F variable.
echo $C ($F);
```

Output: 32

```
//Call $C passing getF () function as a parameter
echo $C (getF (95));
```

Output: 35
What is closure? A closure is a function that can access variables outside the scope in which it was created.
For example, function convert ($f) from the following example returns an anonymous function and that anonymous function can access the $f variable that exists outside the scope of that anonymous function.

```
$F=90;
```

```
// Create a Closure
function convert ($f) {
   return function () use($f) {
   echo(round(($f-32)* (5/9),0));
  };
}

$converter = convert ($F);

$converter ();
```

Output: 32
Another closure example. An anonymous function assigned to the $convertToC variable accessing the $n variable declared outside the function scope.

```
// Create a number
$n = 32;

// Create a Closure
$convertToC = function ($ft) use  ($n) {
return  ( ($ft - $n) * 5/9);
};

echo $convertToC (95); //
```

Output: 35
The next example demonstrates using partial function. In PHP a partial function is originated from a function with multiple parameters.
Original function:

```
$cube = function  ($w, $h, $l) {

return $w * $h* $l;

};
```

A Partial function:

```
$partial_function1 = function  ($width) use  ($cube) {
```

```
return $cube ($width, 3, 5);

};

echo $partial_function1 (2);
```

Output: 30
In the previous example a partial function took one parameter of three. It is possible to use a partial function that takes 2 or all three parameters.

```
$partial_function2 = function ($w, $h) use ($cube) {

return $cube ($w, $h, 7);

};

echo $partial_function2 (2, 3);
```

Output: 42
The partial function example with all three parameters.

```
$partial_function3 = function ($a, $b, $c) use ($cube) {

return $cube ($a, $b, $c);
    };
}
echo $partial_function3 (2, 3, 9);
```

Output: 54
Lambda functions and closures are new for PHP, but they have been widely used in JavaScript, especially in jQuery for a long time. These new PHP features offer developers even more flexibility.

PHP: Migrating from Mysql to Oracle

How to switch from MySQL to Oracle? This tutorial provides some useful tips. In the MySQL database you have a usernames table. Using phpMyAdmin, you can export the "create table usernames" statement and copy it to the notepad. It looks like the following:

```
CREATE TABLE IF NOT EXISTS ùsernames`(
ùseridìnt (11) NOT NULL AUTO_INCREMENT,
`lastnamè varchar (15) NOT NULL DEFAULT '',
`firstnamè varchar (15) NOT NULL DEFAULT '',
ùsernamè varchar (20) NOT NULL DEFAULT '',
`password` varchar (50) NOT NULL DEFAULT '',
èmail` varchar (100) NOT NULL DEFAULT '',
`rolè varchar (20) NOT NULL DEFAULT '',
`dob` datetime DEFAULT NULL,
àddress` varchar (50) NOT NULL DEFAULT '',
`city` varchar (20) NOT NULL DEFAULT '',
`statè varchar (2) NOT NULL DEFAULT '',
`zip` varchar (10) NOT NULL DEFAULT '',
PRIMARY KEY (ùserid`)
) ENGINE=MyISAM DEFAULT CHARSET=latin1
AUTO_INCREMENT=1;
```

You can recreate the same table in Oracle Using Oracle SQL Plus; however, the syntax of the create table statement in the Oracle database will be slightly different from that in MySQL.
For instance, Oracle doesn't have the AUTO_INCREMENT attribute. MySQL adds one auto generated, unique number to the auto incremented field, but in Oracle, we will define this field as a number. A new 'create table' statement for an Oracle database looks like the following:

```
CREATE TABLE usernames (
 userid NUMBER (11),
 lastname VARCHAR2 (20),
 firstname VARCHAR2 (20),
 username VARCHAR2 (20),
 password VARCHAR2 (50) NOT NULL,
```

```
email VARCHAR2 (100) NOT NULL,
role VARCHAR2 (20) NOT NULL,
dob DATE,
address VARCHAR2 (50),
city VARCHAR2 (20),
state VARCHAR2 (2),
zip VARCHAR2 (10),
CONSTRAINT pk_usernames PRIMARY KEY(userid)
);
```

Execute the "create table usernames" statement in Oracle SQL Plus and then execute commit command:
commit;

Now, to add the auto increment to the userid field in the Oracle table you have to create a sequence:

```
create sequence usernames_seq
start with 1
increment by 1
nomaxvalue;
```

Execute the create sequence statement in Oracle SQL Plus and then execute the commit command:
commit;

You may create a trigger:

```
create trigger usernames_trigger
before insert on usernames
for each row
begin
select usernames_seq.nextval into :new.userid
from dual;
end;
```

Now, in your insert query you may use usernames_seq. nextval in place of userid value and it will be auto incremented.

```
insert into usernames
values(usernames_seq.nextval, 'Smith',
```

```
'James', 'secret', 'jamess@yahoo.com', 'admin',
'29-JAN-01','12 West 15 Street', 'Dunedin', 'FL',
'34697');
```

You can view your sequences and triggers by executing the following query in SQL Plus:
select sequence_name from user_sequences;
select trigger_name from user_triggers;
You can disable or enable your triggers by executing the following query in SQL Plus: alter trigger usernames_trigger disable;
alter trigger usernsmes_trigger enable;
One more thing you have to fix in your insert query is the date format.
In MySQL the date is saved as '2001-01-29' in Oracle it is saved as '29-JAN-01'

Compare MySQL insert statement and Oracle insert statement:
MySQL:

```
insert into usernames values (0, 'Smith',
 'James', 'secret', 'jamess@yahoo.com', 'admin',
'2001-01-29',
'12 West 15 STREET', 'Dunedin', 'FL', '34697');
```

Oracle:

```
 insert into usernames values
(usernames_seq.nextval, 'Smith', 'James',
'secret', 'jamess@yahoo.com', 'admin',
'29-JAN-01','12 West 15 STREET', 'Dunedin', 'FL',
'34697');
```

In PHP code you can use the strtotime function to convert time from the MySQL format to the Oracle format:
$dob = date ('d-M-y', strtotime ($dob));

Or you can leave the MySQL date format as it is, but then you have to use in your insert statement you have to use:

```
TO_DATE (<string>, '<format>') function:
```

```
insert into usernames values (0, 'Smith',
'James', 'secret', 'jamess@yahoo.com', 'admin',
to_date (
'2001-01-29:12:00:00AM', 'yyyy-mm-
dd:hh:mi:ssam'),
'12 west 15 STREET','Dunedin','FL','34697');
```

If you want to insert your records using SQL Plus, then you can change the session by using the following command:
alter session set nls_date_format='YYYY-MM-DD';

Commit the changes and use insert statement from MySQL as it is.

```
insert into usernames values (0, 'Smith',
'James', 'secret', 'jamess@yahoo.com', 'admin',
'2001-01-29','12 west 15 STREET', 'Dunedin',
'FL', '34697');
```

Connection to The Oracle Database

To connect to the MySQL database, we use the following parameters:

```
<?php
$hostname = "localhost";
$dbuser = "myuser";
$dbpassword = "secret";
$dbname = "mydb";

$link = mysqli_connect ($hostname, $dbuser, $dbpassword,
$dbname);

if(mysqli_connect_errno())
{
$msg="Failed to connect to MySQL: ".
mysqli_connect_error ();
}
?>
```

To connect to the Oracle database, we use the following PHP code:
$conn=oci_connect ($dbuser, $dbpassword, $dbhost);

Where $dbuser is a user, $dbpassword is a password and $dbhost is a connection string.
The Easy Connect string for Oracle 10g is of the form:
[//]host_name [:port] [/service_name].
With Oracle 11g, the syntax is:
[//]host_name [:port] [/service_name] [:server_type] [/instance_name]. Service names can be found by running the Oracle utility lsnrctl status on the database server machine.

The http://PHP.net website is a good reference for Oracle functions.

Connection string example:
**$dbhost=" (DESCRIPTION= (ADDRESS_LIST= (ADDRESS= (PROTOCOL=TCP)
(HOST=myOracleDB) (PORT=1521))) (CONNECT_DATA= (
SERVICE_NAME=myOracleDB.mydomain.com)
(SERVER=DEDICATED)))";**

On my Windows PC I have the following connection string:
$mydb="
**(DESCRIPTION =
(ADDRESS = (PROTOCOL = TCP) (HOST =
mycomputer_name) (PORT = 1521))
(CONNECT_DATA =
(SERVER = DEDICATED)
(SERVICE_NAME = XE)
)
)";**

```
 $myuser="user";
 $mypassword="secret";

 $conn=oci_connect ($myuser, $mypassword, $mydb);

 //Check if connection is created!
 if(!$conn) {
 $e = oci_error (); // For oci_connect errors
pass no handle
 echo "if no connection<br>";
```

```
 echo htmlentities ($e ['message']);
 } else {
 //Select all users from usernames
 $sql="select * from usernames order by
username";
 $stmt = oci_parse ($conn, $sql);
 oci_execute ($stmt, OCI_DEFAULT);

 while ($row = oci_fetch_array ($stmt, OCI_BOTH))
{
    $userid=$row [0];
    $lastname=$row [1];
    $firstname=$row [2];
    $username=$row [3];
    $password=$row [4];
    $email=$row [5];
    $role=$row [6];
    $dob=$row [7];
    $address=$row [8];
    $city=$row [9];
    $state=$row [10];
    $zip=$row [11];
}

   if ($stmt)
   oci_free_statement ($stmt);

   if ($conn)
   oci_close ($conn);
}
```

When you use the OCI_BOTH oci_fetch_array () mode, you can use the column name as the output array index:
$username=$row ['username'];

Inserting data in the Oracle database

Here is an insert code example. First, you must create an oracle connection.
To connect to the Oracle database, we use the following PHP code:

```
 //Check if connection is created:
if(!$conn=oci_connect($dbuser, $dbpassword,
$dbhost)){
 $e = oci_error (); // For oci_connect errors
pass no handle
 echo "if not connection<br>";
 echo htmlentities ($e ['message']);
 }
 else
 {
 $isql="insert into usernames values
(usernames_seq.nextval,'Smith', 'James','secret',
'jamess@yahoo.com','admin','29-JAN-01','12 west
15 STREET', 'Dunedin', 'FL', '34697');

      $stmt = oci_parse ($conn, $isql);
      $rc=oci_execute ($stmt);
      if (!$rc){
      $e=oci_error ($stmt);
      var_dump ($e);
     }
 oci_commit ($conn);
 oci_free_statement ($stmt);
 }
 oci_close ($conn);
```

Binding a PHP variable to an Oracle placeholder

Binding a variable to an Oracle placeholder is an efficient way to insert data into an Oracle table. The data associated with a bounded variable is never treated as part of the SQL statement and, as a result, it reduces the possibility of an SQL Injection. In addition, it increases performance.

Do not use magic_quotes_gpc or addslashes () when you use oci_bind_by_name () as no quoting is needed. The "oci_bind_by_name ()" inserts data without removing quotes or escape characters.

```
 $isql="insert into (userid, lastname, firstname,
username, password, email, role, dob, address,
city, state, zip)
 Values
```

```
  (:userid_bv, :lastname_bv, :firstname_bv,
:username_bv, :password_bv, :email_bv, :role_bv,
:dob_bv, :address_bv, :city_bv, :state_bv,
:zip_bv)";

 $stmt = oci_parse ($conn, $isql);

 $userid=7;
 $lastname='Smith';
 $firstname='John';
 $username='johns;
 $password='password';
 $email='johns@yahoo.com';
 $role='user';
 $dob='10-MAR-09';
 $address='12 East 19 street';
 $city='New York';
 $state='NY';
 $zip='11200';

 oci_bind_by_name ($stmt, ":userid", $userid
 oci_bind_by_name ($stmt, ":lastname_bv",
$lastname);
 oci_bind_by_name ($stmt, ":firstname_bv",
$firstname);
 oci_bind_by_name ($stmt, "username_bv",
$username);
 oci_bind_by_name ($stmt, ":password_bv",
$password);
 oci_bind_by_name ($stmt, ":email_bv", $email);
 oci_bind_by_name ($stmt, ":role_bv", $role);
 oci_bind_by_name ($stmt, ":dob_bv", $dob);
 oci_bind_by_name ($stmt,
":address_bv",$address);
 oci_bind_by_name ($stmt, ":city_bv", $city);
 oci_bind_by_name ($stmt, ":state_bv",$state);
 oci_bind_by_name ($stmt, ":zip_bv",$zip);

 $rc=oci_execute ($stmt);

 if(!$rc){
 $e=oci_error ($stmt);
 var_dump ($e);
```

```
}
oci_commit ($conn);
oci_free_statement ($stmt);
oci_close ($conn);
```

Using Oci_Bind_By_Name for Updating Records

To update a record in an Oracle table with PHP, use by binding a PHP variable to an Oracle placeholder, as it is a more efficient and safer way. The following is an example of updating a user email address:

```
$usql="update usernames set email=:email_bv
where

username=:username_bv";
$stmt = oci_parse ($conn, $usql);
$username='johns;
$email='johns@gmail.com';

oci_bind_by_name ($stmt, ":username_bv",
$username);

oci_bind_by_name ($stmt, ":email_bv", $email);

$rc = oci_execute ($stmt);

if (!$rc){

$e=oci_error ($stmt);

var_dump ($e);

}

oci_commit ($conn);
oci_free_statement ($stmt);
oci_close ($conn);
```

Using PDO to access the Oracle database

PDO is a Database Access Abstraction Layer, an application programming interface which unifies the communication between a computer application and different databases. In this chapter we will discuss how to use PDO with Oracle.

On my PC I use XAMPP as a webserver. It includes Apache, PHP and MySQL. You can find many tutorials about the installation and use of XAMPP. In the htdocs directory of the XAMPP directory, create the Oracle directory to store all PHP files related to learning PDO with Oracle. Then to run a php file you have to type in the URL: http://localhost/oracle/yourfile.php.

Read a tutorial "How to Use XAMPP to Run Your Own Web Server."
https://blog.udemy.com/xampp-tutorial

Install the Oracle Database 11g Express Edition on your PC
http://www.oracle.com/technetwork/database/database-technologies/express-edition/overview/index.html

oracle client: instantclient-basic-nt-11.2.0.4.0.zip
http://www.oracle.com/technetwork/topics/winsoft-085727.html

While installing the Oracle database, you will be prompted to enter username and password. Write it down for the future use.

After installation of the Oracle Database and client, open the tnsnames.ora file and edit the connection string.

I installed Oracle in "C:/oracle" directory and my tnsnames.ora is located in
"C:/oracle/app/oracle/product/11.2/server/network/ADMIN/tnsnames.ora" directory.

Edit host to your computer name.

XE = (DESCRIPTION = (ADDRESS = (PROTOCOL = TCP) (HOST = mycomputer_name) (PORT = 1521)) (CONNECT_DATA = (SERVER = DEDICATED) (SERVICE_NAME = XE)))

Open the command prompt and type: "sqlplus". Below is a copy from my command prompt window:

```
Microsoft Windows [Version 6.3.9600]
© 2013 Microsoft Corporation. All rights
reserved.
```

```
C:\Users\Sergey>sqlplus

SQL*Plus: Release 11.2.0.2.0 Production on Sat
Feb 25 21:30:31 2017

Copyright (c) 1982, 2014, Oracle. All rights
reserved.

Enter user-name: sergey
Enter password:

Connected to:
Oracle Database 11g Express Edition Release
11.2.0.2.0 - 64bit Production
```

Now you can copy and paste the following create table statement to create your myusernames table.

```
CREATE TABLE myusernames (
usernameid NUMBER (11),
lastname VARCHAR2 (20),
firstname VARCHAR2 (20),
username VARCHAR2 (20),
password VARCHAR2 (50) NOT NULL,
email VARCHAR2 (100) NOT NULL,
role VARCHAR2 (20) NOT NULL,
active NUMBER (4),
CONSTRAINT pk_emp PRIMARY KEY (usernameid)
);
```

After creating the table, create a sequence to use it as the autoincrement id field.

```
CREATE SEQUENCE myusernames_seq
MINVALUE 1
START WITH 1
INCREMENT BY 1
NOCACHE;
```

Create a connect.php file with code for PDO connection to the Oracle database. On my PC it looks like this:

```
<?php
```

```
//connect.php file code start

$mydb="
     (DESCRIPTION =
         (ADDRESS = (PROTOCOL = TCP) (HOST = your
computer name) (PORT = 1521))
         (CONNECT_DATA =
            (SERVER = DEDICATED)
            (SERVICE_NAME = XE)
        )
    )";

    $conn_username = "your username";
    $conn_password = "your password";

    $opt = [PDO:  ATTR_ERRMODE => PDO:
ERRMODE_EXCEPTION,
           PDO:  ATTR_DEFAULT_FETCH_MODE => PDO:
FETCH_NUM,];

    try{
           $conn = new PDO ("oci:dbname=".$mydb,
$conn_username, $conn_password, $opt);
    }
catch (PDOException $e){
           echo ($e->getMessage ());
    }
?>
```

Now, let´s insert users in the myusernames table.
pdo_insert_users.php

```
<?php
//pdo_insert_users

include ('connect.php');
 $sql="insert into myusernames(usernameid,
lastname, firstname, username, password, email,
role, active) values
  (myusernames_seq.nextval, :lastname,
:firstname, :username, :password, :email, :role,
:active)";
```

```
try {

$stmt = $conn->prepare ($sql);

//$id=5;
$lastname='Williams';
$firstname='James';
$username='jamesw';
$password='5f4dcc3b5aa765d61d8327deb882cf99';
$email='myemail.gmail.com';
$role='user';
$active=1;

$stmt->bindParam (':lastname', $lastname);
$stmt->bindParam (':firstname', $firstname);
$stmt->bindParam (':username', $username);
$stmt->bindParam (':password', $password);
$stmt->bindParam (':email', $email);
$stmt->bindParam (':role', $role);
$stmt->bindParam (':active', $active);

$stmt->execute ();

echo "New records created successfully";
   }
       catch (PDOException $e)
      {
      echo "Error: " . $e->getMessage ();
      }
?>
```

The myusernames_seq.nextval sequence will be increased by one after inserting each record.

After inserting a few records, we can try to view our users.

pdo_select_users.php

```
<?php
 //pdo_select_users

 include ('connect.php');

   try{
```

```
            $stmt = $conn->query ('select
usernameid, lastnames, firstname, username, email
FROM myusernames');

            while($row = $stmt->fetch ())
            {
 echo $row[0].",".$row[1]. ", " .$row[2].", ".
$row[3].", " .$row[4]."<br>";
            }

        }catch (PDOException $e){
         echo ($e->getMessage ());
        }
 ?>
```

Misspell a column name to produce an error. For example, change "lastname" to "lastnames". The error message will be displayed.
SQLSTATE [HY000]: General error: 904 OCIStmtExecute: ORA-00904: "LASTNAMES": invalid identifier (ext\pdo_oci\oci_statement.c:148)

If you comment try/catch statements, the message will be:

Fatal error: Uncaught exception 'PDOException' with message 'SQLSTATE [HY000]:
General error: 904 OCIStmtExecute: ORA-00904: "LASTNAMES": invalid identifier (ext\pdo_oci\oci_statement.c:148)' in
C:\xampp\htdocs\oracle\pdo_select_users.php:8 Stack trace: #0
C:\xampp\htdocs\oracle\pdo_select_users.php (8): PDO->query ('select username...')
#1 {main} thrown in
C:\xampp\htdocs\oracle\pdo_select_users.php on line 8

In the php.ini file, set display_errors=off and log_errors=on on the live server and set display_errors=on and error_reporting on a development server.
Now, let´s update a user record.
pdo_update-user.php

```
<?php
 //pdo_update_users

 include ('connect.php');

 $username='jamesw';
 $role='admin';

 try {

 $stmt3 = $conn->prepare ('UPDATE myusernames SET
role= :role WHERE username = :username');
 $stmt3->execute (['role' => $role, 'username' =>
$username]);

        echo "The records updated successfully";
        }
        catch (PDOException $e)
        {
        echo "Error: " . $e->getMessage ();
        }
 ?>
```

To delete a user, use the following code:

```
 <?php
 //pdo_delete_users

 include ('connect.php');

 $username='jamesw';

 try {

 $stmt3 = $conn->prepare ('delete from
myusernames WHERE username = :username');
 $stmt3->execute (['username' => $username]);

        echo "The records deleted successfully";
        }
        catch (PDOException $e)
        {
```

```
        echo "Error: " . $e->getMessage ();
        }
 ?>
```

About using PDO with MySQL, you can read the following tutorial: (The only proper) PDO tutorial (about using PDO with MySQL)
href="https://phpdelusions.net/pdo#why

Call Oracle Procedures or Function

The difference between functions and procedures is that Oracle functions returns only one value, while procedures can have multiple OUT parameters.

Example 1. Oracle procedure: insert_instructor:

```
CREATE OR REPLACE PROCEDURE insert_instructor (
pLast_name IN VARCHAR2, pFirst_name IN VARCHAR2,
pEmail IN VARCHAR2, pPhone IN VARCHAR2, pHiredate
IN DATE, pRate IN NUMBER, pStreet IN VARCHAR2,
pCity IN VARCHAR2, pState IN VARCHAR2, pZip IN
VARCHAR2, instructor_id OUT NUMBER,)
 IS
-- declare variable for inserted record id.
vl_instructor_id NUMBER;
BEGIN -- add a record to the instructors table.
INSERT INTO instructors (instructorid, last_name,
first_name, email, phone, hiredate, rate, street,
city, STATE, zip))
 VALUES
(instructors_seq. nextval, pLast_name
pFirst_name, pEmail, pPhone, pHiredate, pRate,
pStreet, pCity, pState, pZip)
RETURNING instructorid INTO v_instructor_id;
instructor_id: = vl_instructor_id;
RETURN;
END insert_instructor;
```

Call procedure in PL/SQL:

```
  BEGIN insert_instructor ('Smith', 'John',
'johnsm@amail.com', '727-123-1234', '25-JUN-15',
92, '123 St Mary''s Street', 'Dunedin', 'FL',
'34697'); END;
```

Call procedure in PHP:

```
 <?php

  $myuser="smithjohn ";
$mypassword="Practice7 ";
$mydb=" (DESCRIPTION =  (ADDRESS =  (PROTOCOL =
TCP) (HOST = my_host) (PORT myport))
(CONNECT_DATA =  (SERVICE_NAME =
my_oracle_user.my_host)))";
if (!$myconn=oci_connect ($myuser, $mypassword,
$mydb)) {
$e = oci_error (); echo "if not connection<br>";
echo htmlentities ($e ['message']);
} else
{
$query1="BEGIN INSERT_INSTRUCTOR (:last_name,
:first_name, :email, :phone, :hiredate, :rate,
:street, :city, :state, :zip, :instructorid);
end;";
$stmt1 = oci_parse ($myconn, $query1);

$lastname='Willams';
$firstname='Bob';
$email="bobw@yahoo.com";
$phone="727-123-1234";
$hiredate="01-JAN-15";
$rate=80;
$street="423 Druid Rd.";
$city="Clearwater";
$state="FL";
$zip="33756";

oci_bind_by_name ($stmt1, ":instructorid",
$instructorid, 10);
```

```
oci_bind_by_name ($stmt1, ":lastname",
$lastname);
oci_bind_by_name ($stmt1, ":firstname",
$firstname);
oci_bind_by_name ($stmt1, ":phone", $phone);
oci_bind_by_name ($stmt1, ":hiredate",
$hiredate);
oci_bind_by_name ($stmt1, ":rate", $rate);
oci_bind_by_name ($stmt1, ":street", $street);
 oci_bind_by_name ($stmt1, ":city", $city);
oci_bind_by_name ($stmt1, ": state ", $ state);
oci_bind_by_name ($stmt1, ":zip", $zip);
$er1=oci_execute ($stmt1);

if (!$er1)
{
 $e = oci_error ($stmt1);
 echo $e ['message'];
}
$ret1=oci_commit ($myconn);

echo "Instructor ID=". $instructorid;
} //if connected
```

Example 2. Oracle Function: 'insert_instructor'.

```
  CREATE OR REPLACE FUNCTION insert_instructor (
pLast_name IN VARCHAR2, pFirst_name IN VARCHAR2,
pEmail IN VARCHAR2, pPhone IN VARCHAR2, pHiredate
IN DATE, pRate IN NUMBER, pStreet IN VARCHAR2,
pCity IN VARCHAR2, pState IN VARCHAR2, pZip IN
VARCHAR2)
RETURN number IS RESULT number;
BEGIN INSERT INTO instructors
(instructorid, last_name, first_name, email,
phone, hiredate, rate, street, city, STATE, zip)
VALUES
(instructors_seq.nextval, pLast_name,
pFirst_name, pEmail, pPhone, pHiredate, pRate,
pStreet, pCity, pState, pZip)
RETURNING instructorid INTO RESULT;
```

Call the function 'insert_instructor' in PHP

```
<?php

$query2="BEGIN :result := INSERT_INSTRUCTOR (
:last_name, :first_name, :email, :phone,
:hiredate, :rate, :street, :city, :state, :zip);
end;"; $stmt2 = oci_parse  ($myconn, $query2);
$lastname='Willams'; $firstname='Bob';
$email="bobw@yahoo.com"; $phone="727-123-1234";
$hiredate="01-JAN-15"; $rate=80; $street="423
Druid Rd." $city="Clearwater"; $state="FL";
$zip="33756";

oci_bind_by_name ($stmt2, ":result", $result,
10);
oci_bind_by_name ($stmt2, ":lastname",
$lastname);
oci_bind_by_name ($stmt2, ":firstname",
$firstname);
oci_bind_by_name ($stmt2, ":phone", $phone);
oci_bind_by_name ($stmt2, ":hiredate",
$hiredate);
oci_bind_by_name ($stmt2, ":rate", $rate);
oci_bind_by_name ($stmt2, ":street", $street);
oci_bind_by_name ($stmt2, ":city", $city);
oci_bind_by_name ($stmt2, ":state ", $state);
oci_bind_by_name ($stmt2, ":zip", $zip);
$er2=oci_execute ($stmt2);
if(!$er2) {
$e = oci_error ($stmt2);
echo $e ['message'];
}
$ret2=oci_commit($myconn);
echo "Instructor ID=". $result."<br>";
?>
```

Example 3. Oracle procedure: 'update_hiredate'.

This procedure takes in three parameters: last name, first name, and new hire date and takes out one parameter, instructorid.

```
  CREATE OR REPLACE PROCEDURE update_hiredate (
 plastname IN VARCHAR2, pfirstname IN VARCHAR2,
pnew_hiredate IN DATE, pinstructor_id OUT NUMBER)
IS lv_instructorid NUMBER;
BEGIN UPDATE instructors
SET hiredate= pnew_hiredate WHERE
firstname=pfirstname AND lastname=plastname
RETURNING instructorid INTO lv_instructorid;
pinstructor_id:= lv_instructorid; RETURN; END
update_hiredate;
```

Call the procedure 'update_hiredate' with PHP

```
 <?php

$query3="BEGIN update_hiredate(:last_name,
:first_name, :new_hiredate, :instructor_id)
;end;";
$stmt3 = oci_parse($myconn, $query3);
$lastname="Barry";
$firstname="John";
$new_hiredate="07-FEB-14";
$istructor_id=0;

oci_bind_by_name ($stmt3, ": instructor_id ",
$istructor_id, 10);
oci_bind_by_name ($stmt3, ":last_name",
$lastname);
oci_bind_by_name ($stmt3, ":first_name",
$firstname);
oci_bind_by_name ($stmt3, ":new_hiredate",
$new_hiredate);
$er3=oci_execute ($stmt3);
if (!$er3) {
$e = oci_error ($stmt3);
```

```
echo $e ['message'];
}
$ret3=oci_commit ($myconn);
echo "Instructor_ID=". $istructor_id."<br>";
```

Example 4. Oracle function: 'update_hiredate'.

```
  CREATE OR REPLACE FUNCTION update_hiredate(
plastname IN VARCHAR2, pfirstname IN VARCHAR2,
pnew_hiredate IN DATE) RETURN DATE IS RESULT
DATE;
BEGIN UPDATE instructors SET hiredate=
pnew_hiredate WHERE firstname=pfirstname AND
lastname=plastname
RETURNING hiredate INTO RESULT;
RETURN(RESULT);
END update_hiredate;
```

Call the function 'update_hiredate' with PHP

```
  <?php

$sql4="BEGIN: result:= update_hiredate(
:last_name, :first_name, :new_hiredate);
end;"
 $stmt4 = oci_parse($myconn, $sql4);
$lastname="Barry";
$firstname="John";
$new_hiredate="07-MAR-14";

oci_bind_by_name($stmt4,": result ", $result,
10);
oci_bind_by_name($stmt4, ":last_name",
$lastname);
oci_bind_by_name($stmt4, ":first_name",
$firstname);
oci_bind_by_name($stmt4, ":new_hiredate",
$new_hiredate);
$er4=oci_execute ($stmt4);

 if(!$er4) {
 $e = oci_error ($stmt4);
```

```
 echo $e ['message'];
}
$ret4=oci_commit ($myconn);
echo "New hire date=". $result."<br>";
```

Example 5. Oracle function: 'return_hiredate'.

```
  CREATE OR REPLACE FUNCTION return_hiredate(
pfirstname IN VARCHAR2, plastname IN VARCHAR2)
RETURN DATE IS RESULT DATE;

BEGIN SELECT hiredate INTO RESULT FROM
instructors WHERE lastname = plastname AND
firstname = pfirstname;
RETURN (RESULT);
 END return_hiredate;
```

Call the function 'return_hiredate' with PHP

```
  $query5="BEGIN :result := return_hiredate
(:firstname, :lastname); end;";
$lastname="Barry"; $firstname="John";
$stmt5 = oci_parse ($myconn, $query5);
oci_bind_by_name ($stmt5, ":result", $result,50);
oci_bind_by_name ($stm5t, ":lastname",
$lastname);
oci_bind_by_name ($stmt5, ":firstname",
$firstname);
$er5=oci_execute ($stmt5);
if (!$er5) {
$e = oci_error ($stmt5);
echo $e ['message'];
}
else
{
$ret5=oci_commit ($myconn); echo "hire
date=".$result."<br>";
}
?>
```

Example 6. Oracle procedure 'return_hiredate'.

```
  CREATE OR REPLACE PROCEDURE return_hiredate(
pfirstname IN VARCHAR2, plastname IN VARCHAR2,
pHiredate OUT DATE) IS lv_hiredate DATE;

BEGIN SELECT hiredate INTO lv_hiredate FROM
instructors WHERE lastname = plastname AND
firstname = pfirstname;
pHiredate := lv_hiredate;
RETURN; END return_hiredate;
```

Call the procedure 'return_hiredate' with PHP

```
 <?php
  $query6="BEGIN return_hiredate (:firstname,
:lastname, :hiredate);
 end;";
  $firstname='john';
 $lastname='smith';
 $hiredate="";

 $stmt6=oci_parse($myconn, $query6);

oci_bind_by_name($stmt6,":hiredate",$hiredate,20)
;
oci_bind_by_name($stmt6, ":lastname", $lastname);
oci_bind_by_name($stmt6,":firstname",
$firstname);

  $er6=oci_execute ($stmt6);

  if(!$er6)
  {
  $e = oci_error ($stmt6); echo $e ['message'];
  }
  $ret6=oci_commit ($myconn);
  echo "Hire date=".$hiredate."<br>";
  }
 ?>
```

Example 7. Oracle procedure 'delete_instructor'.

```
  CREATE OR REPLACE PROCEDURE delete_instructor (
plastname IN OUT VARCHAR2, pfirstname IN
VARCHAR2) IS lv_lastname VARCHAR2 (20);
BEGIN DELETE FROM instructors WHERE
lastname=plastname AND firstname=pfirstname
returning lastname INTO lv_lastname;
plastname:=lv_lastname; RETURN; END
delete_instructor;
```

Call the procedure 'delete_instructor' with PHP

```
  <?php
$sql7="BEGIN delete_instructor (:last_name,
:first_name);
end;";
$istmt7 = oci_parse ($myconn, $sql7);
$last_name='Barry';
$first_name='John';

oci_bind_by_name ($istmt7, ":last_name",
$last_name);
oci_bind_by_name ($istmt7, ":first_name",
$first_name);
$er7=oci_execute ($istmt7);
if (!$er7) {
$e = oci_error ($stmt7);
echo $e ['message'];
}
$ret7=oci_commit ($myconn);
echo "last name=". $last_name."<br>";
?>
```

Example 8. Oracle procedure: 'get_instructors'.

This procedure returns a cursor that can hold multiple records and fields.

```
  CREATE OR REPLACE PROCEDURE get_instructors (
plastname IN VARCHAR2, mycurs OUT SYS_REFCURSOR)
IS
```

```
BEGIN OPEN mycurs FOR SELECT lastname, firstname,
email, phone, hiredate, rate, street, city,
STATE, zip FROM instructors WHERE
lastname=plastname; END get_instructors;
```

Call the procedure 'get_instructors' with PHP

```
  <?php
$curs = oci_new_cursor ($myconn);
$lastname="Willams";
$query8="BEGIN get_instructors (:lastname, :curs
);
end;";
$stmt8 = oci_parse ($myconn, $query8);

oci_bind_by_name ($stmt8, ":lastname",
$lastname); oci_bind_by_name ($stmt8, ":curs",
$curs, -1,

OCI_B_CURSOR);
oci_execute ($stmt8);
oci_execute ($curs);
echo "Instructors Records:<br>";
while ($row = oci_fetch_array ($curs, OCI_NUM)) {
$last_name=$row [0];
$first_name=$row [1];
$email=$row [2];
$phone=$row [3];
$hiredate=$row [4];
$rate=$row [5];
$street=$row [6];
$city=$row [7];
$state=$row [8];
$zip=$row [9];
echo $last_name.' '.$first_name.' '.$email.'
'.$phone.' '.$hiredate.' '.$rate.' '.$street.'
'.$city.' '.$state.' '.$zip.'<br>'; }
oci_free_statement ($stmt8);
oci_free_statement ($curs);
oci_close ($myconn);
?>
```

Example 9. Oracle procedure 'delete_instructor2'.

**CREATE OR REPLACE FUNCTION delete_instructor2 (plastname IN VARCHAR) RETURN SYS_REFCURSOR AS my_cursor SYS_REFCURSOR;
BEGIN OPEN my_cursor FOR SELECT * FROM instructors WHERE lastname=plastname; DELETE FROM instructors WHERE lastname=plastname; RETURN my_cursor; END delete_instructor2;**

PHP call the procedure 'delete_instructor2'

```
<?php
$p_curs = oci_new_cursor ($myconn);
$lastname="Tom";
$query9="BEGIN :curs := delete_instructor2
(:lastname); end;";
$stmt9 = oci_parse ($myconn, $query9);

oci_bind_by_name ($stmt9, ":lastname",
$lastname); oci_bind_by_name ($stmt9, ':curs',
$p_curs, -1, OCI_B_CURSOR); // Execute Statement
oci_execute ($stmt9);
oci_execute ($p_curs, OCI_DEFAULT);
echo "Deleted Records:<br>";
while($row = oci_fetch_array ($p_curs, OCI_NUM)){
$last_name=$row [0];
$first_name=$row [1];
$email=$row [2];
$phone=$row [3];
$hiredate=$row [4];
$rate=$row [5];
$street=$row [6];
$city=$row [7];
$state=$row [8];
$zip=$row [9];
echo $last_name.' '.$first_name.' '.$email.'
'.$phone.' '.$hiredate.' '.$rate.' '.$street.'
'.$city.' '.$state.' '.$zip.'<br>';
}
oci_commit($myconn);
oci_free_statement ($stmt9);
```

```
oci_free_statement ($p_curs);
oci_close ($myconn);
```

Appendix: Installation of Apache & PHP

Download Apache 2.2.22 web server for Windows from **http://**httpd**.apache.org**
Be certain to select binaries for Windows and not a source code. There are two kinds of files to choose from, one with openssl and one with no-ssl. Select the one having no-ssl, download and save it to your desktop, and click to start it running. The Open File-security Warning dialog is opened. Click the Run button.

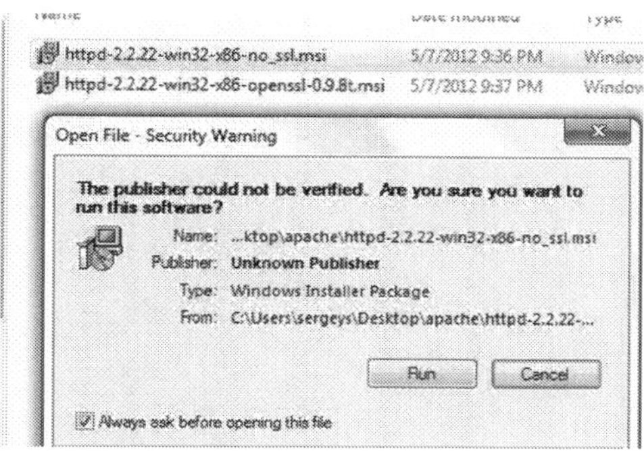

Figure 34. Apache installation.
On the next window enter your server information.
Click the Next button.

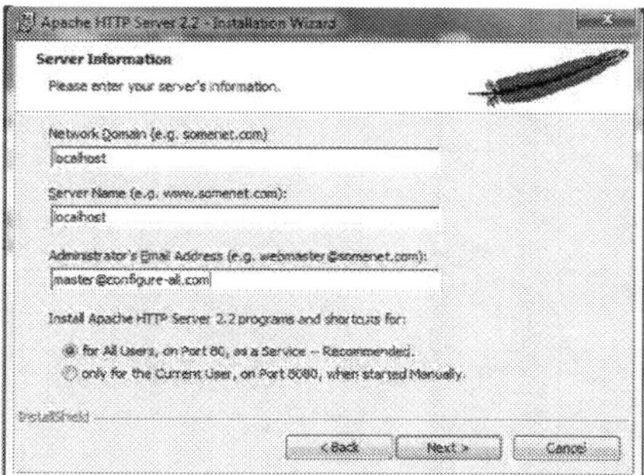

Figure 35. the server information input.

The Typical option in the Select Type window is selected by default. This is OK. Click the Next button.

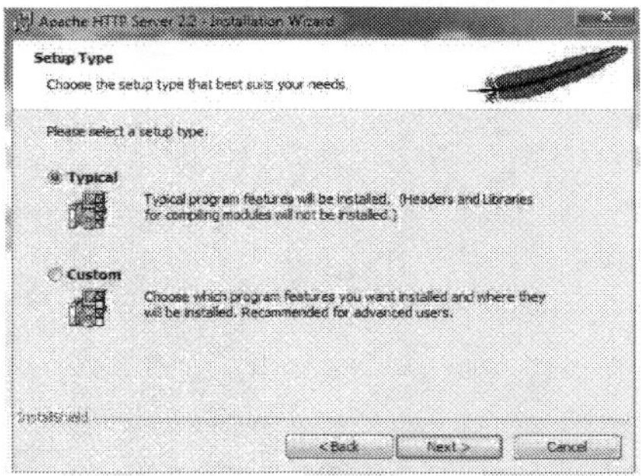

Figure 36. Selecting the installation type.

It is very important that you change the destination folder to C:\Apache2.2.

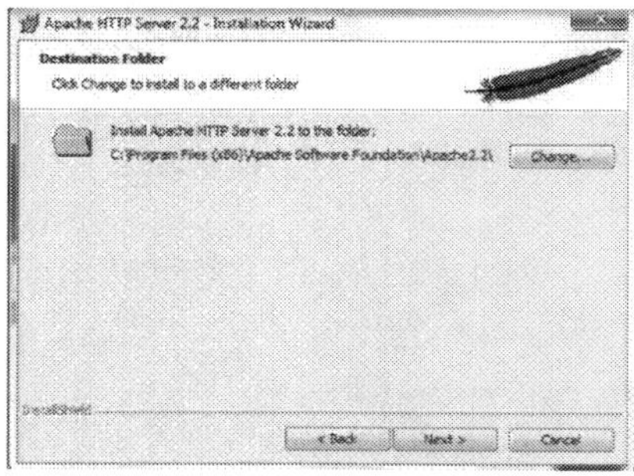

Figure 37. Changing the location.

Click the Next button and the Finish installation window is displayed. Click the Finish button and you're done. If it asks permission to restart your computer, please allow.

Open any browser and type the address http://localhost and hit enter. The It Works text is displayed in the browser. I recommend that you use the last version of Firefox as your default browser for learning PHP programming.

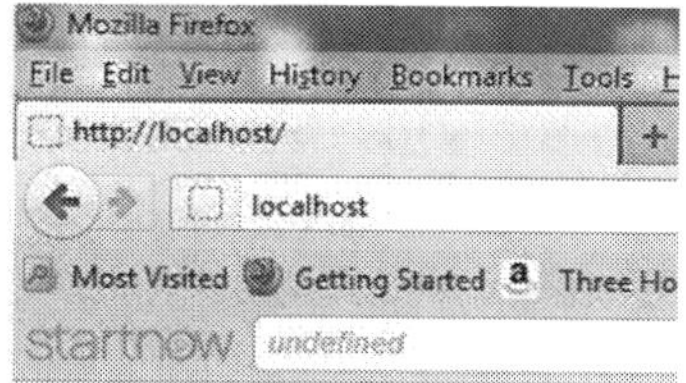

Figure 38. Running a default webpage on the localhost.

Installation of the PHP on Windows

Download PHP from http://windows.php.net/download
At the time of editing this book, the last PHP version is 7.2.4.
Read "Which version do I choose?" on the download page.
Select the Thread Safe and choose a zip file option.
Save it on your desktop and extract files to the C:\php folder.

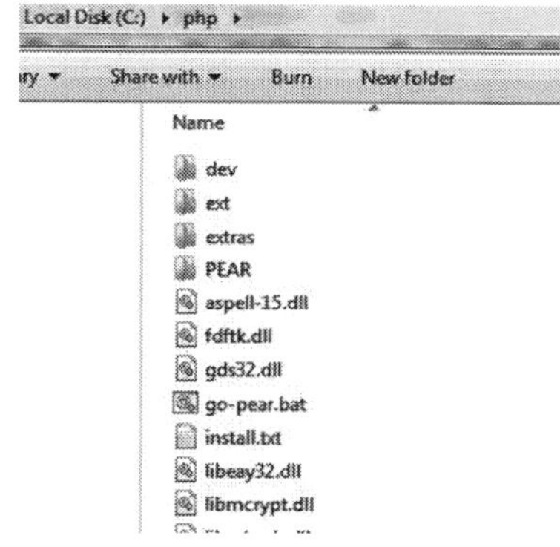

Figure 39. The PHP directory after installation.

Go to My Computer or Windows Explorer and open the Apache2.2 folder.
Open the conf folder and open the httpd.conf file in notepad, textpad, or in notepad ++.

In the httpd.conf file, find the line beginning with "LoadModulo" and add the following lines of text as follows:

```
LoadModule php5_module c:/php/php5apache2_2.dll
 ScriptAlias /php/ "c:/php/"
```

```
 AddType application/x-httpd-php .html .phtml
 AddType application/x-httpd-php. php4
 AddType application/x-httpd-php. php
 DirectoryIndex index.html index.html.var
index.php
```

Save the above httpd.conf file.
Open the C:\php folder and php.ini. recommended file in the notepad. Find the following line, and set it to your extension directory:
; Directory in which the loadable extensions (modules) reside.

```
extension_dir = "./"
```

It appears in the following manner on my PC:

```
extension_dir = "C:\php\ext"
```

Find the line:

```
;upload_tmp_dir =
```

Type the directory to which your user will be permitted to upload files.
On my PC it is the following:

```
upload_tmp_dir = "c:\Apache2\htdocs\upload"
```

Uncomment

```
# php.MySQL.dll
```

If you want to use a short open php tag like "<?" instead of **"<?php" Set "short_open_tag" to On.**

```
short_open_tag = On
```

By default, it is set to Off in the PHP.INI file. In the event the hosting server does not support the short open tag, it is recommended you use the "<?php" tag.
Make sure that the following extensions are uncommented in the PHP.INI file. By default, they are commented, preceded by a semicolon as in the following:
; extension=php_curl.dll

To uncomment the line, delete leading semicolon.

extension=php_curl.dll
extension=php_gd2.dll
extension=php_gettext.dll
extension=php_imap.dll
extension=php_mbstring.dll
extension=php_mcrypt.dll
extension=php_mysql.dll
extension=php_mysqli.dll
extension=php_pdo.dll
extension=php_pdo_mysql.dll
extension=php_pdo_sqlite.dll
extension=php_xmlrpc.dll
extension=php_zip.dll

Rename the php.ini.dist file to php.ini and copy it to the Windows\system32 directory.
Copy php5ts.dll from "C:\php" to "C:\Apache2.2/bin".
Create a test directory in C:\Apache2\htdocs directory.
Open notepad and type a php script:

```
<?php

 phpinfo ();

 ?>
```

Save file as phpInfo.php in the test directory.
Start the Apache web server from the Windows start up menu.
Open your Internet Explorer and type in the following URL address:
http:/localhost/

If Apache installed and configured correctly, the Apache home page displays.
To test php installation and configuration, type the following URL address in the browser:
`http:/localhost/test/phpinfo.php` and hit enter.
The following page is displayed:

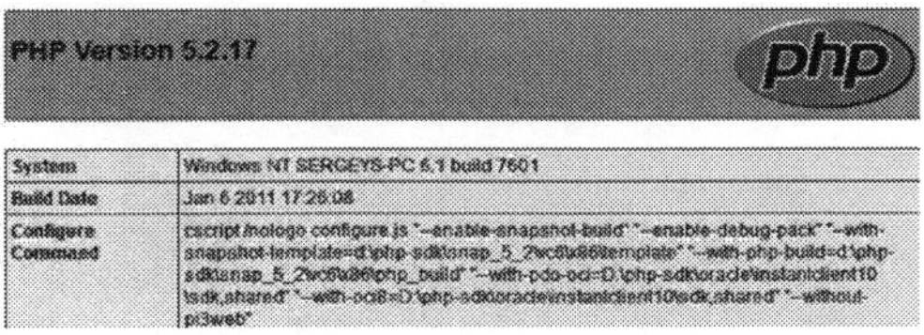

PHP Version 5.2.17

System	Windows NT SERGEYS-PC 6.1 build 7601
Build Date	Jan 6 2011 17:26:08
Configure Command	cscript /nologo configure.js "--enable-snapshot-build" "--enable-debug-pack" "--with-snapshot-template=d:\php-sdk\snap_5_2\vc6\x86\template" "--with-php-build=d:\php-sdk\snap_5_2\vc6\x86\php_build" "--with-pdo-oci=D:\php-sdk\oracle\instantclient10\sdk,shared" "--with-oci8=D:\php-sdk\oracle\instantclient10\sdk,shared" "--without-pi3web"

Figure 40. PHP info page.

If the PHP code is displayed in the browser, restart your computer. If the code still appears, reread the instructions to check for what you may have missed.

Each time you modify the PHP.INI file, you must restart Apache so that changes take effect.

Virtual Server Setup

Here we´ll learn to configure Apache for virtual server setup.

If you´ve developed several websites on your local PC, it is convenient to create a separate virtual server for each website.

On my PC, Apache is installed in the c:/Apache2.2 directory. Yours may be installed in a different location. Nevertheless, find the conf directory inside the Apache directory and open the httpd.conf file in Notepad. Scroll down to the end of the file and type a directive for a virtual server. Below are two virtual server examples with IP address´ 127.0.0.2 and 127.0.0.3. You can create as many virtual servers as you wish using the following template example:

```
NameVirtualHost 127.0.0.2
<VirtualHost 127.0.0.2>
<directory /sitea/htdocs>
allow from all
</directory>
ServerAdmin admin@sitea
ServerName 127.0.0.2
DocumentRoot "/sitea/htdocs"
ScriptAlias /cgi-bin/ "sitea/cgi-bin/"
ErrorLog /sitea/error.log
CustomLog /sitea/access.log common
</VirtualHost>
```

```
NameVirtualHost 127.0.0.3
<VirtualHost 127.0.0.3>
<directory /siteb/htdocs>
allow from all
</directory>
ServerAdmin admin@siteb
ServerName 127.0.0.3
DocumentRoot "/siteb/htdocs"
ScriptAlias /cgi-bin/ "siteb/cgi-bin/"
ErrorLog /siteb/error.log
CustomLog /siteb/access.log common
</VirtualHost>
```

I created the sitea/htdocs and siteb/htdocs directories on the C drive and placed an index.html file in each htdocs directory.

For Site A, I typed the following line of html code in the index.html: <h1>Site A</h1>.

In index.html for Site B, I typed in the following line of html code: <h1>Site B</h1> Restart Apache, open browser and type in the URL http://127.0.0.2 and press enter.

The browser displays the text: Site A.

Type http://127.0.0.3 and press enter. The browser displays the text: Site B

You can place a PHP file in each root (htdocs) directory and run it. Now you have the ability to develop two separate websites.

Installation of the XAMPP on Windows

XAMPP is an easy to install Apache distribution containing MySQL, PHP, and Perl. Download it from https://sourceforge.net/projects/xampp

Create an xampp folder in the root directory and save executable xampp-win32-7.1.8-0-VC14-installer.exe in the folder.

Select the executable file, right click your mouse and select "Run as Administrator".

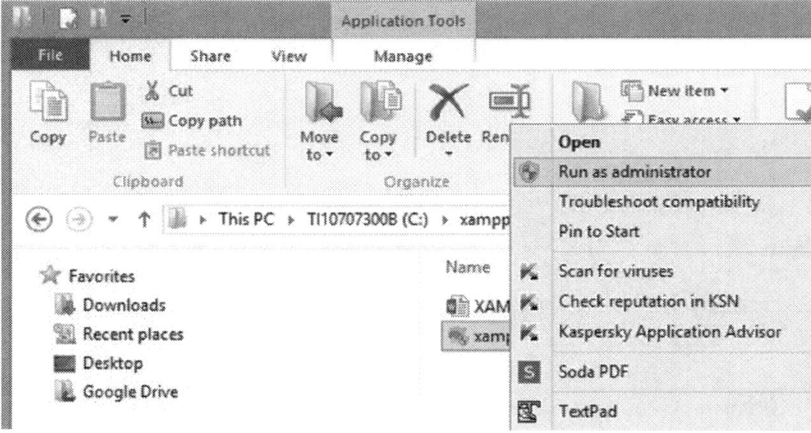

Figure 41. Run as Administrator.

If you have an anti-virus software, you may need to pause protection or disable it temporarily.

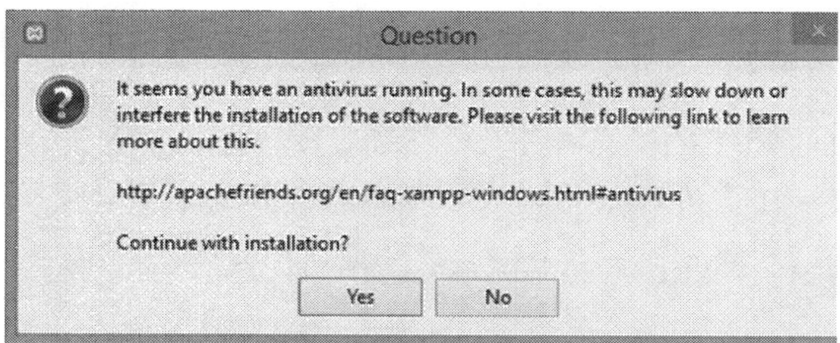

Figure 42. Disable anti-virus.

Do not change default selections.

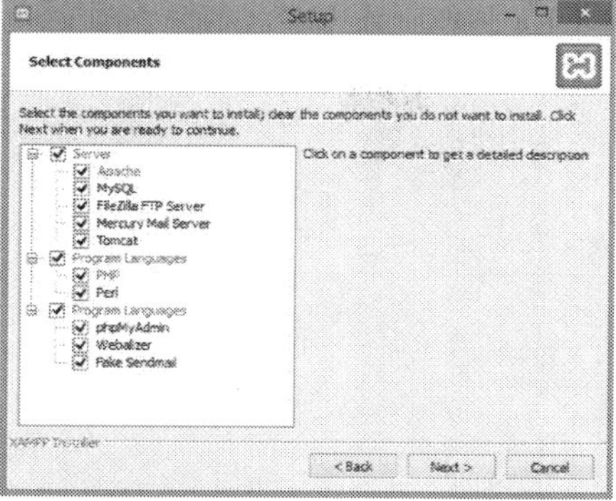

Figure 43. Default selections.

Change the destination directory from C:\Program Files (x86) to C:\xampp7

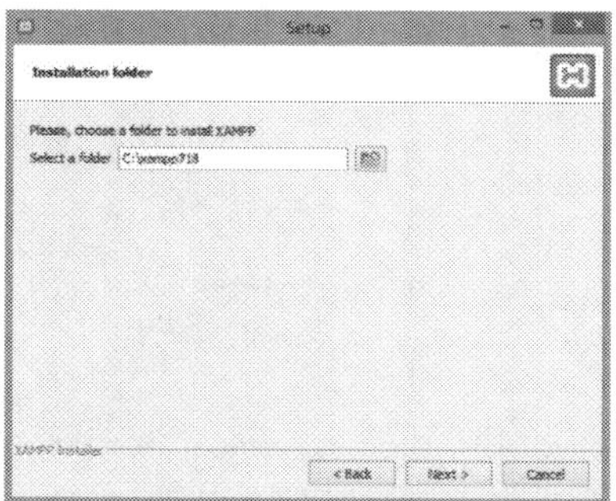

Figure 37. The installation directory. Just click Next.

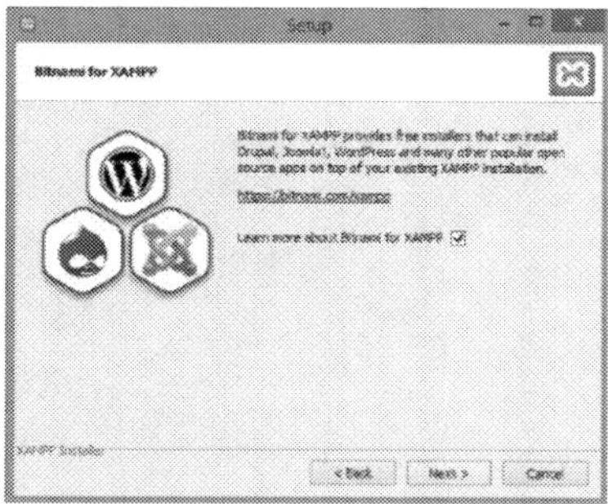

Figure 44. Just click Next.

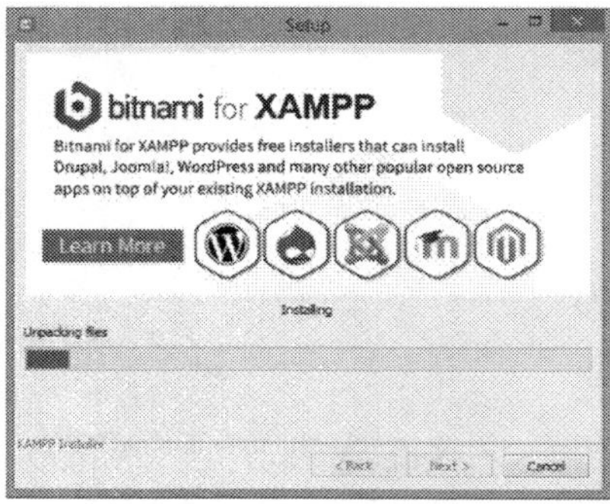

Figure 45. Just click Next.

Figure 46. Just click Finish.

Find the icon XAMPP in your start menu and open it

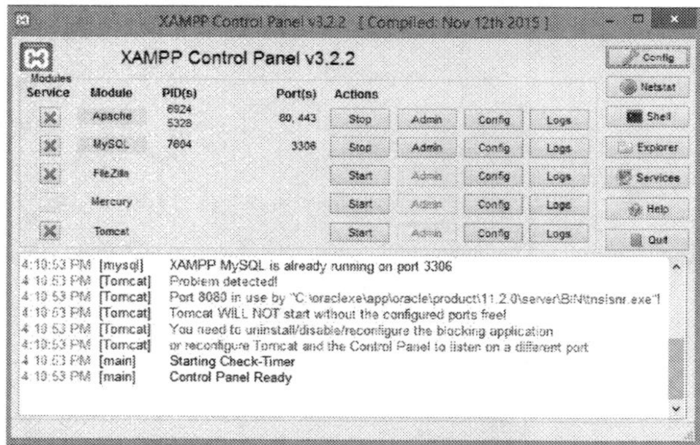

Figure 47. XAMPP control Panel

The XAMPP control panel is displayed. Click start Apache then after Apache has started running, click Start MySQL. MySQL should start running.

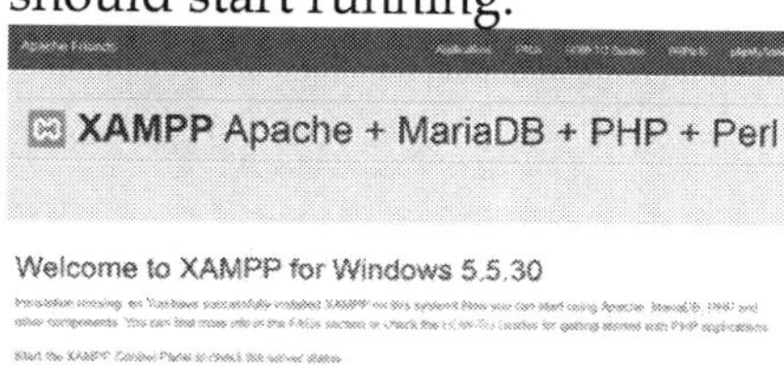

Figure 48. The welcome page.

Open your favorite browser and type in the URL "http://localhost/" The welcome page is displayed.

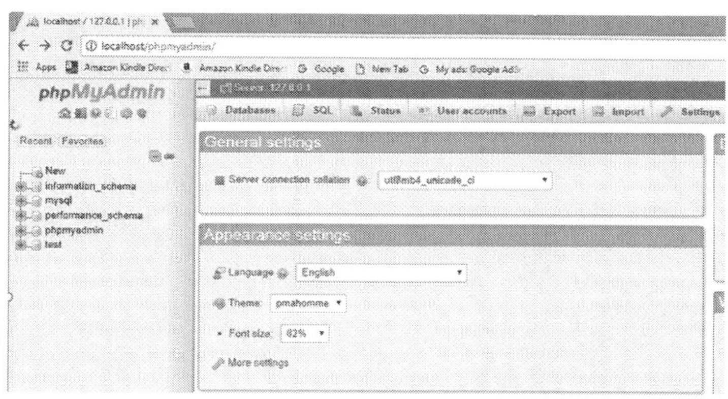

Figure 49. phpMyAdmin.

Click the phpMyAdmin link in the right upper corner. phpMyAdmin is started.

If your phpMyAdmin displays an error, it may be related to port conflict with another software running on your PC. You may change the default 3306 port used by MySQL in the xampp\mysql\bin\my.ini file to the 3307 port.

Restart Apache, MySQL and XAMPP each time after changing a port.

To change the port for phpMyAdmin, open the config.default.php file located in the "phpMyAdmin\libraries" directory.

Find a line: $cfg ['Servers'] [$i] ['port'] = '' and enter between single quotation marks a mysql port that is displayed on the XAMPP Control Panel.

phpMyAdmin home page. You can click the SQL button on the main menu. In the text area, type a query "create database mydb" and click the Go button. The mydb database will be created.

To create a visitor table, select a database on the left and click SQL. In the text area, type or paste a create table statement and click the Go button. The visitors table will be created.

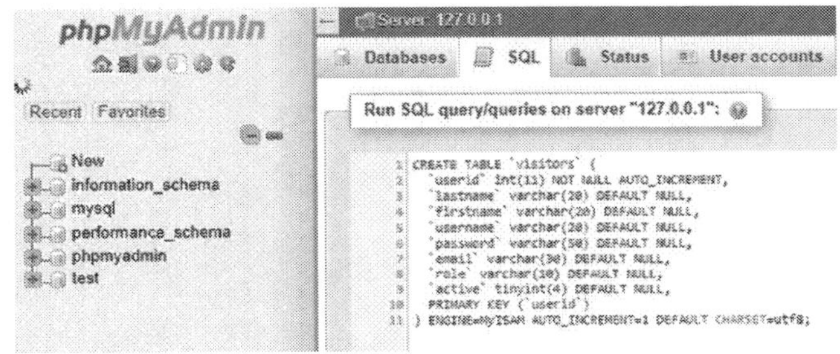

Figure 50. Create visitors table.

Click the Structure button on the main menu and you will see the table structure: the table fields, data type and the size.

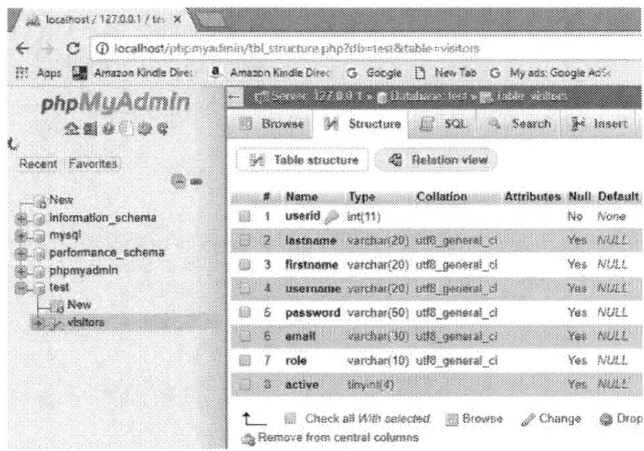

Figure 51. The table structure.

To insert a record to the visitors table, select a table on the left and click the Insert button on the main menu. In the list of fields, enter a visitor´s data and click the Go button. The record will be inserted.

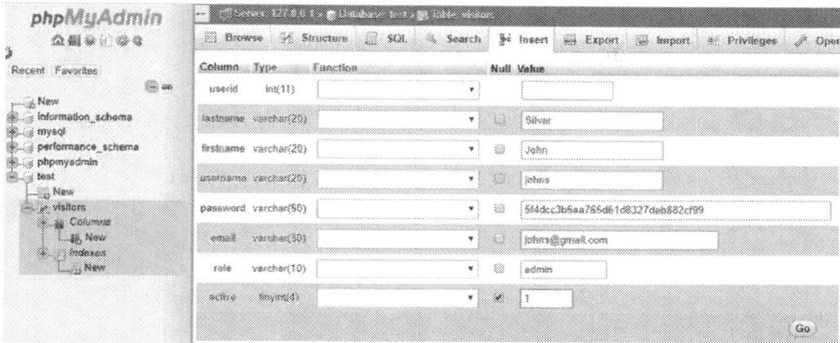

Figure 52. Insert a record.

Click the Browse button and the records inserted in the table will be displayed.

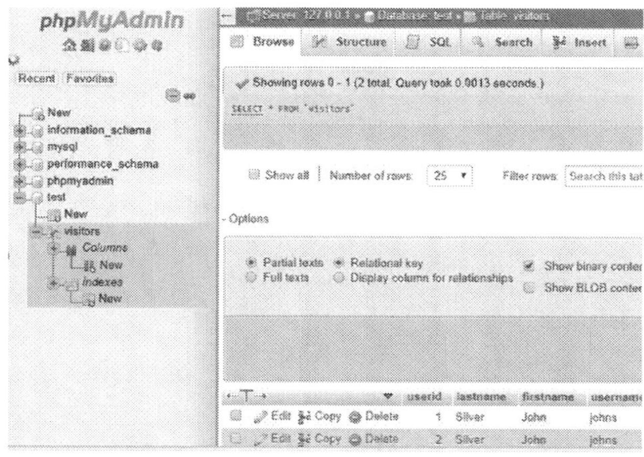

Figure 53. The records are displayed.

To export table structure and table data, click the Export button on the main menu. Enter table name in the new template text box, select it in the existing template list and click the Go button.

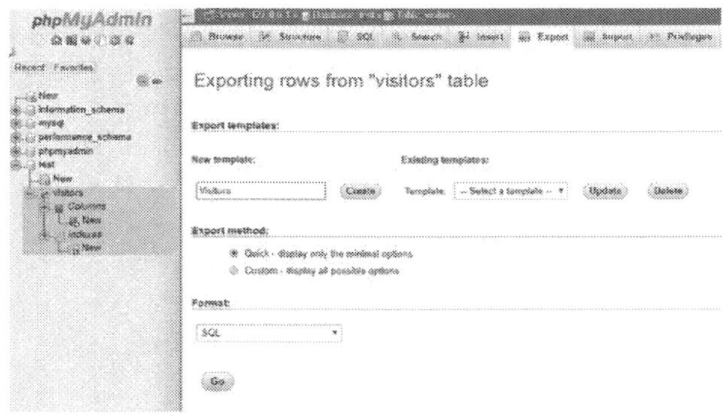

Figure 54. Export a table.

The Save dialog is displayed. Save the file

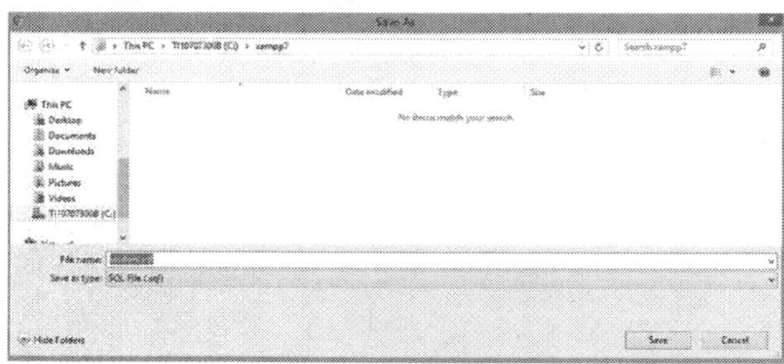

Figure 55. Save the exported script.

Open the sql file and it will include the create table statement for the visitors table.

```
CREATE TABLE visitors(
userid int(11) NOT NULL AUTO_INCREMENT,
lastname varchar(20) DEFAULT NULL,
firstname varchar(20) DEFAULT NULL,
username varchar(20) DEFAULT NULL,
password varchar(50) DEFAULT NULL,
email varchar(30) DEFAULT NULL,
role varchar(10) DEFAULT NULL,
active tinyint(4) default NULL,
primary key(userid)
```

) ENGINE=MyISAM AUTO_INCREMENT=1 DEFAULT CHARSET=utf8;

Using the XAMPP Shell

Click the button on the XAMPP control panel.

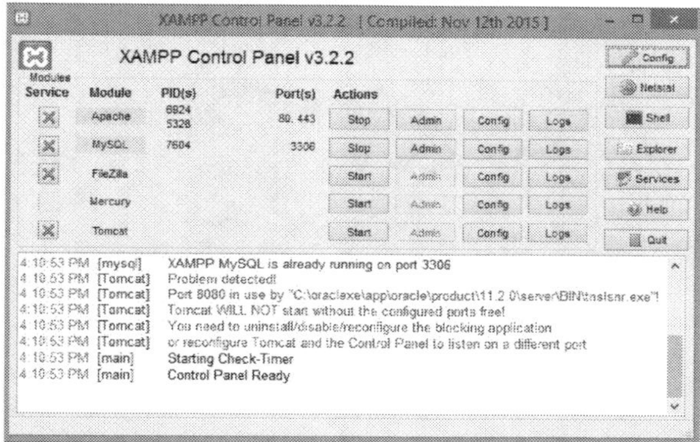

Figure 56. Control Panel.

Login to MySQL with the root user. View exiting databases with the "SHOW DATABASES" command.

```
MariaDB [(none)]> show databases;
+--------------------+
| Database           |
+--------------------+
| information_schema |
| mysql              |
| test               |
+--------------------+
3 rows in set (0.03 sec)

MariaDB [(none)]> _
```

Figure 57. Show databases.

```
MariaDB [mydb]> use mysql
Database changed
MariaDB [mysql]> CREATE USER 'johns'@'localhost' IDENTIFIED BY 'Password@7';
Query OK, 0 rows affected (0.17 sec)

MariaDB [mysql]> GRANT ALL PRIVILEGES ON mydb.visitors TO 'johns'@'localhost' ID
ENTIFIED BY 'Password@7';
Query OK, 0 rows affected (0.09 sec)

MariaDB [mysql]> _
```

Figure 57. Create a user "johns" with password "Password7@".

```
MariaDB [(none)]>
MariaDB [(none)]> GRANT ALL PRIVILEGES ON mysql.* TO 'johns'@'localhost' IDENTIF
IED BY 'Password@7';
Query OK, 0 rows affected (0.05 sec)

MariaDB [(none)]> exit
Bye

Sergey@SERGEYSK c:\xampp
# mysql -u johns -pPassword@7
Welcome to the MariaDB monitor.  Commands end with ; or \g.
Your MariaDB connection id is 7
Server version: 10.0.17-MariaDB mariadb.org binary distribution

Copyright (c) 2000, 2015, Oracle, MariaDB Corporation Ab and others.

Type 'help;' or '\h' for help. Type '\c' to clear the current input statement.

MariaDB [(none)]>
```

Figure 58. Grant user with all privileges.

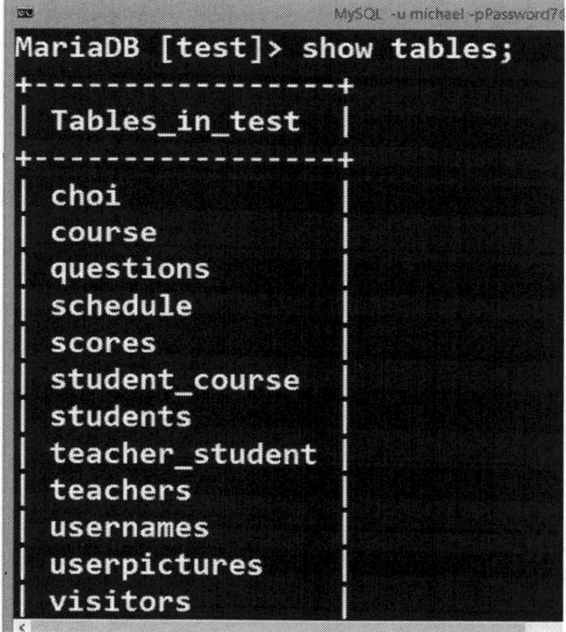

Figure 59. Show tables.

Select a database with the command "use test".
To see existing tables, type "SHOW TABLES";

```
MariaDB [test]> show fields from visitors;
+-----------+-------------+------+-----+--------
| Field     | Type        | Null | Key | Default
+-----------+-------------+------+-----+--------
| userid    | int(11)     | NO   | PRI | NULL
| lastname  | varchar(20) | YES  |     | NULL
| firstname | varchar(20) | YES  |     | NULL
| username  | varchar(20) | YES  |     | NULL
| password  | varchar(50) | YES  |     | NULL
| email     | varchar(30) | YES  |     | NULL
| role      | varchar(10) | YES  |     | NULL
| active    | tinyint(4)  | YES  |     | NULL
+-----------+-------------+------+-----+--------
8 rows in set (0.12 sec)
```

Figure 60. Display columns of the visitors table.

```
MariaDB [test]> insert into visitors(userid, lastname,
    -> firstname, username, password, email, active)
    -> values (0, 'Smith', 'John','johns','Bear@&',
    -> 'johns@gmail.com',1);
Query OK, 1 row affected (0.01 sec)
```

Figure 61. Insert a visitor´s record.

```
MariaDB [test]> update visitors set role='admin'
    -> where userid=4;
Query OK, 1 row affected (0.02 sec)
Rows matched: 1  Changed: 1  Warnings: 0

MariaDB [test]> Select userid, firstname, lastname
    -> from visitors;
+--------+-----------+-----------+
| userid | firstname | lastname  |
+--------+-----------+-----------+
|      1 | Johnson   | Silverson |
|      2 | John      | Smith     |
|      3 | Peter     | Willams   |
|      4 | Sergey    | Skudaev   |
+--------+-----------+-----------+
4 rows in set (0.00 sec)
```

Figure 62. Update the visitor's record.

```
MariaDB [test]> select userid, firstname, lastname
    -> from visitors order by lastname;
+--------+-----------+-----------+
| userid | firstname | lastname  |
+--------+-----------+-----------+
|      1 | Johnson   | Silverson |
|      4 | Sergey    | Skudaev   |
|      5 | John      | Smith     |
|      3 | Peter     | Willams   |
+--------+-----------+-----------+
4 rows in set (0.04 sec)
```

Figure 63. Display records from the visitors table.

Delete a visitor.

```
MariaDB [test]> delete from visitors
    -> where lastname='Smith';
Query OK, 1 row affected (0.00 sec)

MariaDB [test]> select username, firstname, lastname
    -> from visitors;
+----------+-----------+-----------+
| username | firstname | lastname  |
+----------+-----------+-----------+
| johns    | Johnson   | Silverson |
| peterw   | Peter     | Willams   |
| sergeys  | Sergey    | Skudaev   |
+----------+-----------+-----------+
3 rows in set (0.00 sec)
```

Figure 64. Delete a visitor.

The records are selected and then one of the records is deleted. Now you know how to use the shell.

Download all the PHP code examples used in this book:
http://www.learn-coding.today/phpbook/phpbook.zip

PHP Resources:

www.sitepoint.com
PHP Tutorial - W3Schools
www.codetoad.com
www.phpfreaks.com
www.devx.com
www.phpclasses.org
www.zend.com
http://dev.mysql.com/tech-resources

My Websites

http://learn-coding.today
http://hardstuffez.com

Sign Up for free code examples
http://www.learn-coding.today/code_from_serge.php

My eBooks on Amazon.com

Sergey Skudaev

C++ Programming By Examples
PHP Programming for Beginners
Learn SQL by Examples
The Ultimate eBook Creator

Roy Sawyer

Chemistry for Students and Parents
The Easiest Way To Understand Algebra
Geometry For Students and Parents

ABOUT THE AUTHOR

Sergey Skudaev is currently living in Florida.
He obtained a master's degree in biology from a foreign University, where he specialized in neuropsychology. He also has a degree in Computer Science from Borough of Manhattan Community College, which he attained after moving to the US.
Since then, Sergey has been working as a software quality engineer and web developer for a computer company in Florida.
He has more than ten years of teaching experience and a long-standing interest in new computer technologies, psychology, and brain physiology.
When he has some time to relax, Sergey enjoys swimming in the ocean off the Florida coast or going for walks with his dog. He also enjoys traveling, particularly in the USA.
You can contact Sergey at support@learn-coding.today

Made in the USA
Middletown, DE
30 November 2023